Fritz Wetherbee

TAKEN FOR GRANITE

Fritz Wetherbee's

NEW HAMPSHIRE

Fritz Wetherbee

PLAIDSWEDE PUBLISHING
Concord, New Hampshire

ISBN-13: 978-0-9790784-8-4
Library of Congress Control Number: 2008936391

Designed and composed in Minion Pro
at Hobblebush Books,
Brookline, New Hampshire (www.hobblebush.com)

Printed in the United States of America

Published by:

PLAIDSWEDE PUBLISHING
P.O. Box 269 · Concord, New Hampshire 03302-0269
www.plaidswede.com

CONTENTS

THE PEOPLE

THE WETHERBEES

ACKNOWLEDGMENTS

I WANT TO THANK the following for their support of my work and this book:

Mary Ann Mroczka, senior producer, *New Hampshire Chronicle,* WMUR-TV

Jeff Bartlett, general manager, WMUR-TV

Hearst Arguyle, for allowing me to do this book

Rick Broussard, editor of *New Hampshire Magazine,* who got this project under way

Holly Scopa, Tracey Spolter, Donna Smith, Tom Griffith and Tiffany Eddy, Chris Shepherd, Chris McDevitt, Paul Falco, Chris Orr, Ryan Murphy and the rest of the *Chronicle* gang who make my on-air job easy

John Gulardo of Langdon (N.H.), who took the best picture of me I've ever had

George Geers and Sara Minette of Plaidswede Publishing Co.

Laura for her love, support and suggestions

— Fritz Wetherbee

INTRODUCTION

FRITZ WETHERBEE KNOWS how to dig into history and bring up gold. Not big clunking chunks of gold, but little bits that sparkle, small stories of small towns that introduce us to colorful characters, take us to remote locations, recount events that might be forgotten, and preserve the essence of this state we love so much.

As a storyteller, I travel town to town telling and gathering tales, just as Fritz travels town to town gathering tales to tell on "New Hampshire Chronicle" and put in this priceless series of books.

New Hampshire lives in these Fritz Wetherbee books.

Because Fritz and I are both in the business of New Hampshire stories, people often ask if I know him. "I do," I brag. "I've even shared a stage with him a time or two." They are always impressed. As they should be. Often they add: "We love Fritz."

At the Toadstool in Milford a couple of years back, hawking my book, I took a stroll around the store during a break. An older man sat in the corner reading Fritz's latest. A younger man, his son I think, asked what he was doing. "There's a story in here about Milford!" the older man said proudly.

In New Hampshire, connections matter. To open a book and find a story about your own town, that's a thrill. Yup, Fritz Wetherbee writes thrillers.

This native, whose roots in the state go back several generations, is an icon—*and* a good writer. He is, in fact, beloved in the state of

New Hampshire, by me and many others who appreciate all he does to preserve and liven up our history. His stories are inevitably lively, often humorous, and always to the point. His many fans, including me, recognize the genius of a simple, true, well-told story.

Thanks, Fritz. Keep up the good work.

—Rebecca Rule,
New Hampshire author and humorist

THE STORIES

The Cornet Solo

AMOS ROWELL PLAYED second cornet in the Kensington Town Band back before the Civil War.

When the war came, the entire band was drafted and went off to provide marching music and entertainment for the Union troops.

Amos' brother was also in the war and was shot and killed in action.

At the end of the war, just before the band came home to Kensington, it played a concert in Washington, D.C.

By this time Amos had become first cornet.

The band played "Be It Ever So Humble, There's No Place Like Home," and Amos' solo on the cornet was so appreciated by the crowd that they insisted he do an encore of the piece. There wasn't a dry eye in the house. It was the high point of his career.

But three years in the Union army, traveling with the troops at the front lines, had taken its toll. Amos was worn out.

When he came back to Kensington, he found that his wife, whom he had left three years before, had run up debts. She was, the town history says, "frivolous."

Amos was worn out. His health was gone, and he could not pay his wife's debts. (In those days, a wife was not responsible for money matters in a family.) And the merchant who pressed charges was a former friend of his.

So Amos Rowell was thrown in the Portsmouth jail. After a few months he contracted consumption, which is what they called tuber-culosis back then. He died in jail.

At the funeral the widow, in a fit of grief and remorse, howled like a dog and actually threw herself into the grave atop her husband's coffin.

And that was that. A young man who gave his all for his country came home to a silly wife, a greedy friend, a cruel justice system, imprisonment and early death.

Oh, and there is one other thing.

The concert where Amos played his cornet solo . . . that concert was at Ford's Theater. The band played before the play went on . . . the play during which the president was assassinated.

For you see, Amos Rowell's beautiful solo was the last music Abraham Lincoln ever heard. ❧

Amoskeag Canal

Fritz stands alongside the Amoskeag Canal in Manchester.

IN THE EARLY days of New Hampshire, everything was on the water. All the towns and settlements were on the water. If you had to get anywhere, you sailed.

If you had stuff to sell, you put it on a boat. It was the easiest and cheapest way to move goods. If you wanted to go from Dover to Boston, you sailed. Heck, if you wanted to go from Dover to Exeter, you sailed.

The Merrimack River was the major way into the interior of New Hampshire.

The falls in Lawrence and Lowell and Manchester were perfect places for mills, but it was impossible to get a boat of any size by the dams. So the only boats able to get way upstream were those small enough to be carried around the rapids, like canoes.

Canals were needed to get around those rapids.

So, by the end of the eighteenth century, men were starting to construct canals around all the major falls on the Merrimack River.

In the spring of 1794, Judge Samuel Blodget set about building a mile-and-a-quarter-long canal on the east side of the river in Manchester. It was all hand dug. Human labor. It took five years to complete.

The upper end of the canal was just down from the Amoskeag Bridge where the dam was constructed using the huge natural stones in the river. On the east side a mill pond was formed which flowed into the start of the canal. Just a few feet inside was the first lock, and barges loaded with lumber or bricks or fur would sail into the lock to be lowered to the next level.

At the time of the canal construction, there were already two mills at the outflow of the pond—a gristmill and a lumber mill belonging to the Blodget family.

The first gates of the canal were an invention of Judge Blodget. The gates would be opened downstream by the velocity of the barge going through it. In other words, a self-opening gate. That was fine in theory.

The problem was, the boats went too fast and, instead of opening the gates, the boats stove them in. Add to this, a great freshet—a spring flood—occurred in 1799 that flushed away everything.

But, like everything else in this world, sooner or later the best way would be found, and so it was with the Amoskeag Canal.

In 1808 the greatest canal construction in the history of America up to that time opened. No, not the Erie Canal; that would not be completed for another 18 years. No, this was the Middlesex Canal. It ran twenty-seven miles northwest through Middlesex County in Massachusetts.

It began at the Charles River in Boston and joined the Merrimack River just above Lowell. It was then, and for the next fifty years, possible to travel by boat from downtown Boston to downtown Concord, New Hampshire, with canal rides around Nashua and Hooksett and Bow.

The canal around Manchester was improved as the Amoskeag Mill was improved. By the time of the Civil War, it was the largest mill in the world, with a total floor space larger than the Pentagon.

Later, the canals were used to supply the water power to the various buildings. By then the railroad had supplanted the barges to carry goods to and from the mill.

Over the years, the canal became two canals, one for upriver and one for downriver, and they were there for all to see until the 1970s. One canal ran right beside Canal Street and the other is today the middle street of The Mill Yard. But, in the end, the canals had no use other than being fun to look at. And they were smelly and dangerous, and they were finally filled in.

So the next time you drive through The Mill Yard, take a minute and think to yourself, "Hey, this used to be water." ❧

Bound Rock

This sign in Seabrook marks the story of Bound Rock.

BACK IN THE 1930S, the Army Corps of Engineers was moving some earth in Seabrook when it uncovered a rock. Carved into the top of the stone was a date: "A.D. 1657."

It was historic. Turned out this was the original stone that marked the boundary between New Hampshire and Massachusetts.

Forty years before the stone was placed, representatives of the towns of Hampton and Colchester met and agreed that the boundary between the towns should start at the mouth of the Hampton River. However, the boundary was not to disturb the land in Hampton encompassing the Bachelor farm. (Seabrook was back then a part of Hampton and Salisbury, Massachusetts, was then called Colchester.)

Then, in 1657, the line was laid out again from the same rock, and this time the date was carved in its top.

Back in the seventeenth century this rock was at the mouth of the Hampton River. But over the years, the course of the river moved. The rock, though, stayed in the same place.

And although it isn't in the river anymore, it is still under water.

It is hard to see now, but you will find it under a grate in a protective chamber made of concrete. ✒

The Church of Nashua 1679

THE FIRST MINISTER in what is now the city of Nashua was the Reverend Thomas Weld. He came to his church about 1679.

Back then all the land in the city and for miles around was part of the township of Dunstable.

I own a history of the old town of Dunstable. It was written by Charles J. Fox in 1846, a time when there were many veterans still alive in Nashua who fought in the Revolution.

Now church life in Dunstable was dreary back when Reverend Weld arrived. The history tells us that dancing at weddings was forbidden. Women were forbidden to put ribbons in their hair; it was considered superstitious. A young man named William Walker was put in jail for an entire month because he went courting a maid before he asked permission from her parents. It was also forbidden to "keep Christmas" as it was "a Popish Custom," a term meaning of Catholics.

The church was a plain affair. Right in front of the pulpit was an elevated chair where the ruling elder sat. There were no pews but rather plain benches. Women on one side, men on the other. Children were at the back of the hall.

There was even a law against standing up in church to leave before the blessing was completed. If one turned his or her back on the minister before the service was completed, it was considered "profane" and the culprit would be confined in a cage set near the meeting-house. The cage was strictly for those who offended the sanctity of the Sabbath. Those who missed meeting for three months were publicly whipped.

The settlers of Dunstable, in their petition to become a town, described themselves as "of sober and orderly conversation."

One has no doubt they were telling the truth. ☙

The Buckhorn Tree

IN THE NORTHERNMOST point in the town of Pittsfield, there where the towns of Pittsfield, Loudon, Gilmanton and Barnstead meet, there once stood a giant willow tree. It was called "The Buckhorn Tree." It stood for a hundred years marking the spot where the four towns met.

Why it was called "The Buckhorn Tree" and how it came to be a boundary marker is quite a story.

Barnstead had been granted its charter in 1727, but it was many years later that any settlers came.

By then no one knew where the original town survey lines had been drawn. No one knew specifically where the four towns met. The maps had been lost. So the New Hampshire Legislature appointed a committee to ascertain the boundary.

They held hearings, and an old man came forward and said that he could find the spot because he had been in the original survey team that established the line. He had, he said, been a boy of twelve at the time.

"How do you know you can find the line?" the committeemen asked.

Well, it seemed that boy had messed up doing his duties with the team, and the head surveyor had given him a severe beating.

He said that he felt he had been ill-treated and, in revenge, stole the company's bottle of rum and drank it all and hid the empty bottle under a rock beside the surveyed line.

If he could find the old bottle, that would establish the exact point for the town lines.

And so the committee and the old man went to where he felt the bottle might be. They searched only a short while when, eureka!, they found the empty rum bottle.

And the line was re-established.

But, so as not to forget the spot, the committee bored a hole in a willow tree that overgrew the very spot. In this hole they rammed a stag's horn.

And for years people were able to find the spot by locating the old willow with the buckhorn in its trunk.

Sometime around the turn of the twentieth century the old tree began to decay, and finally it blew down in a windstorm. The old buckhorn was removed and for years was in the possession of the Towle family over in Loudon. ❧

Universalist Meeting

IN COLONIAL TIMES, in order to become a town, the population of that place was required to build a meetinghouse and hire a settled minister.

Back then there were only three religions in the state: Congregationalist, Presbyterian, and Anglican. The citizens in most of New Hampshire's towns were Congregationalists.

So, early on, the general tax money went not only to support roads and schools and the justice system; the general tax money also went to support the only church and minister in the town. As everyone was of the same faith back then, there were few who spoke against spending tax money on religion.

I know it's hard to believe, but in early New Hampshire there were no Catholics.

But then people began to join other sects. And soon New Hampshire had Quakers, Methodists, Baptists and Free Will Baptists, and Jews and, yes, even Catholics. And with these new faiths people began to object to having their tax money spent on religions they did not belong to.

Well, the local government in most New Hampshire towns agreed and would give those who could prove they were a member of another faith an exemption on that percent of their tax that would have gone to the town's minister.

The thing was, you had to prove you were giving money to another faith and that faith had to meet the requirements of the law . . . that is, that it was legitimate.

All that was a preamble to an event that took place in Winchester, back in 1803. That year the national leadership of the Universalist Church held a convention there, the purpose of which was to create for the church, a creed.

Now the Universalists, like the Unitarians, had no creed. They believed that people should be free to worship their God as they saw fit, that they didn't need a creed and that a creed would divide people more than it would bring them together.

Incidentally they also believed in "universal salvation," hence the name of the church. And, as with the Unitarians, they believed in God in one person.

That being neither here nor there for the purposes of our story, suffice it to say the group of ministers from the church (twenty-one in all) were in Winchester to cobble up a creed.

Now why, you may ask, did they need a creed when they didn't believe in creeds?

They needed a creed because without a creed the local government would not give an exemption on their local tax to support the town church and minister. Without a creed a sect did not meet the requirements.

So for a couple days the ministers, including the famous religious philosopher Hosea Balou, hammered out a creed. And this is it:

"We believe in one God whose nature is love, revealed in one Lord Jesus Christ, by one Holy Spirit of Grace who will finally restore the whole human family to holiness and happiness.

"We believe the scriptures of the Old and New Testaments contain a revelation of the character of God, of the duty, interest, and final destination of mankind.

"We believe that holiness and true happiness are inseparably connected and that believers ought to be careful to maintain order and practice good works for these things are good and profitable to men."

And that was it. Enough to get the faithful some money back.

Incidentally, the Universalists and Unitarians are now one and the same church. But back then, the Unitarians refused to create a creed of any sort.

Not that there's anything wrong with that. ✒

To Market in Winter

WE OFTEN THINK of snow as a terrible impairment to transportation. But in Colonial times, when it came to moving goods, snow was looked upon as a wonderful thing.

Back then there were few highways, and the highways that existed were terrible, filled with rocks or swampy. A journey over those early highways always meant a broken axle or a popped ring on the wagon wheel, not to mention horses stumbling. It was slow going. You even had to find places in the rivers to ford.

But in the winter these same roads were much smoother due to the snowfall. Much larger and heavier loads could be transported on sleds and sledges pulled by oxen. You could pile high the goods. The slippery roads made traveling much faster, and the rivers were frozen over so there were lots of shortcuts.

The bad thing about winter, back then, was a thaw. If you got to a destination and the snow melted, there was nothing to do but wait 'til the snow fell again. Even an empty sledge was too much for a brace of animals to pull on bare ground.

In the early days, there were usually two times in winter when people in the hinterlands sent their goods to market: late January and late February.

The market they went to was usually Portsmouth or Salem, Massachusetts, sometimes Newburyport. Way up north it was often Portland, Maine.

The goods sent to these centers were salt pork, hand-woven fabric or raw wool, or yarn, butter, half-carcasses of hogs frozen stiff, furs, hides, cheese, poultry, beef, dried apples . . . stuff that came from the farm.

In the early days there would be one great load for the entire village. Later there would be a number of sleds with a number of drivers who would travel together.

At first it was all pulled by oxen but, as the roads got better, more and more horses were used, sometimes harnessed together to make four or six pulling one rig.

Food for the journey would often be bean porridge frozen in a tin pail with a small ax to smash pieces of the ice to melt and drink, and pre-cooked, roasted beef to re-heat on an open fire.

On the way to market there were inns where the drivers could stop and get a place to sleep and also use the fireplaces to cook their meals.

These inns, of course, also sold alcohol, and alcohol was a chief source of income. You can imagine living in the wilderness in winter with little to do and then setting out with your buddies on a great adventure. You can bet there was drinking and partying on the way. Their horses would be cared for, and the men would head for the bar.

When there was a great freeze and the roads became ideal for sleds, there would suddenly be a huge migration to market. The road from Henniker and Weare, for instance, would have literally thousands of sleds on the highway. And, yes, I said thousands.

These market rush times continued until just before the Civil War when the railroads were put in. After that, stuff could be sent to market at any time. And within half-a-dozen years, the yearly mid-winter migration to market disappeared. ❧

The Lost Child

THIS STORY HAPPENED a long time ago, in the summer of 1770. Back before we were the United States. It took place about five miles from Drewsville, which is in the northern part of the town of Walpole.

On this particular day, Isaac Cady had left his home to go a few hundred yards into the forest to cut some wood. He left his wife and kids at home. One of the kids was a two-and-a-half-year-old named Jacob. Jacob was cute and precocious, the apple of his parents' eye.

"Go see Papa," Mrs. Cady told the youngster.

And Jacob went off to find his father.

At sunset Isaac came home.

"Where's Jacob?"

"Don't know. I thought he was with you."

So the child was missing.

The Cadys immediately went out searching. They called the child's name. No answer. They sent one of the other children to get help from the neighbors half a mile away. At dawn they still had not found little Isaac.

By this time, there were some four hundred friends and neighbors helping from Drewsville and Alstead and Walpole. All day they searched and into the night. The third day dawned with no word about the child.

By this time, Colonel Benjamin Bellows and Captain John Jennison of Walpole were in charge of the searchers. Even they with their military training could not find Jacob.

Mrs. Cady is quoted in the town history as saying that if she could know that the child was dead and so relieved from suffering (even if the boy was eaten by beasts) if he was not suffering, she could be still. But, she said, "Can I lie down to rest not knowing but my little Jacob is wandering and starving in yonder gloom?" So the mother was resolved.

As nightfall came, Colonel Bellows ordered that bonfires be built at regular intervals within sight of each other, and that the search would continue. Further he said that when the child was found that a gun should be fired to tell the others. And when the child was found dead two gunshots were to be fired. When the child was found alive, three gunshots would be fired.

The third night progressed. Long about ten o'clock the family was startled by a single gunshot.

They waited (it took a while to reload weapons in that day). Then a second shot was heard. They waited again . . . "POW" . . . a third shot!

The boy was alive!

He had been found by Colonel Bellows himself.

The child was found asleep in the moss at the southeast corner of Warren's Pond, hungry but unharmed. He was carried by the colonel himself and was, the history tells us, deposited in the embrace of his delighted parents. ⟡

Freewill Baptists

This is the first church building ever built for the Freewill Baptist faith.

THE SIMPLE, WHITE church on a hilltop a mile or so away from the village of New Durham has great historical significance to people all around the world.

This is the first church building ever built for the Freewill Baptist faith, a religion that has about a million adherents. Nowadays many prefer to be called simply "Free Baptists."

The religious tenants of the Freewill Baptist Church go back to the seventeenth century and are based on the teachings of a theologian who was a contemporary of John Calvin. The theologian was James Arminius. Among other tenets of his doctrine was the conviction that a person's salvation depended greatly on how he or she lived this life.

The Arminian doctrine became popular in America in the North in the late 1700s, when the question of slavery began to be foremost in the nation's consciousness. Arminians, and later the Freewill Baptists, felt that not to speak out on the greatest evil of the time was sinful and would surely be noted by God. In other words, people have the free will to make choices and suffer the consequences if those choices are evil.

The regular Baptist church was strong in the South and at the time took no stand for or against the issue.

Now before there was a Freewill Baptist Church, there were evangelical preachers who traveled around to towns and cities converting people to the Arminian faith. Such a preacher was George Whitefield.

In 1770 Whitefield came to Portsmouth. One of the people who turned out to hear him was a young Congregationalist, Benjamin Randall. Randall was deeply moved; so moved that he converted to the Baptist faith.

But the Calvinistic Baptists did not accept his concept of free will. Soon there was friction with the congregation, and Randall knew that he must move on. Where he moved to was New Durham, which is where he founded a congregation that believed as he did.

In 1780 that congregation put up the church building and became the first-ever to call itself by the name Freewill, the first of its kind in all of America.

In the 1800s, because of the emancipation question, the church was to grow by leaps and bounds and, among other accomplishments, members of the faith were to found a great progressive educational institution, Bates College in Maine. ☙

Dream of Death in Hollis

THERE IS A ghost story that is told in Hollis, which is reputed to be true. I'll tell it and let you decide.

Seems, once upon a time, October of 1758 to be exact, there lived in Hollis a young man named Joseph Flagg. And this young man fell gravely ill. For a number of days he was unconscious and in a fever, and most supposed he would die. But he did not die.

But when Joseph Flagg awoke he confessed that while in the coma he had a dream. "I cannot tell you all the things I saw and heard in my dream," he told his mother. "But this I will tell you: I dreamed that I shall live exactly three years longer."

Well, Joseph Flagg's health returned, and soon he had forgotten his illness. In a year or two he became engaged to a young woman named Sally Eastman, and on the eve of his wedding he rode his horse to her home for a visit. It was October 19, 1761.

Late in the evening his mother heard the galloping sound of horses' hooves and went to the door. It was her son returning. As he dismounted he said, "I have had my call, Mother. I have had my call. I have come home to die."

His mother, of course, was frantic. "What are you saying,?" she asked. "Nothing will hurt you. We will care for you."

But he would not hear it. "Mother," he said. "Mother, I had forgotten. This is my last day on earth."

"No!" his mother said. "That was a sick boy's dream. You must forget it."

"I did forget it," he said. "I was galloping on toward Sally's, thinking of the pleasure we should have at the wedding and the pranks they would play, when suddenly the horse haunted and turned left off the road and went into the churchyard and he stopped at the ash tree just beyond father's grave. I turned him back to the trail but again he went to the churchyard and stopped at the same spot. I have come home to be ready."

His mother then put him to bed and she, herself, mounted the horse and went to a neighbor to have them go and fetch Sally and to alert the doctor.

It was dawn before Joseph's beloved and the doctor arrived. By then the mother was weeping over the still form of her youngest son whose spirit had left him just as dawn was breaking.

His stone reads:

To the memory of Joseph Flagg aged twenty-three
who died October 20, 1761
Erected by Miss Sally Eastman

The Salamander

BACK IN COLONIAL days, there was a particular superstition that people believed wholeheartedly.

This superstition was that if a family could keep a hearth fire going for twenty-five years, on the eve of the twenty-sixth year a salamander would come and eat up the fire.

See back then there were no matches, and a fire in the kitchen hearth was kept going constantly summer and winter. To let the fire go out was bad luck.

And when the salamander came in twenty-five years and ate the fire, it was also bad luck, and it was necessary then to kill the creature.

Well, the story goes that in a town north of Concord in the late 1700s, there was a small home with a hearth that had never let the fire go out. The home was occupied by a couple who lived there alone; their children were grown and gone away.

One day the wife decided to cook a bag pudding.

Now a bag pudding was made by filling the stomach of a sheep with cornmeal mixed with pork and vegetables. The whole meal was then put into an iron pot and boiled over the fire for a few hours.

While the meal was cooking, the wife stepped out of the kitchen for awhile. When she returned, she was startled to see a slimy creature with a tail running from the fire toward the bed. (People, by the way, kept their beds in the kitchen back then, for warmth.) The thing disappeared under the bed.

There were ashes all over the floor and the fire was sputtering. The woman knew what it was immediately. It had been twenty-five years.

It was the salamander.

She called her husband.

"Jacob," she cried, "the fire has burned twenty-five years, and the salamander has come and eaten it up. The salamander is under the bed. Get the ax and kill it!"

Jacob came with the ax.

The trail of ashes led from the fire to the bed.

Jacob took a shovel and prodded the creature as he held the ax. It appeared, and he chopped.

A burst of greasy guts exploded on the floor, and the two looked.

What they saw was this: the pudding.

It was then they noticed that the crane that held the boiling pot had broken and had spilled the liquid into the fire, putting it out. The wife had come in the door just in time to see the pudding, now covered with feathers from the floor and ashes from the fireplace, rolling under the bed. The string that tied the whole thing up looked like a tail.

And so it was that the family dog got a great salamander meal that night.

And the family . . . ate beans. ✒

The Big Elm

THE LEGEND OF the Big Elm is told in the Langdon Town History. This is it:

Back during the French and Indian War, a detachment of soldiers came north from Boston. They were attempting to catch up with their regiment. The regiment was marching toward Quebec and had a two-day's start. The men in the detachment were marching at double time.

On their third day, they passed through what is now the town of Langdon. Here one of their men fell sick and was left in the care of a local Indian tribe. Well, the young soldier got better and soon fell in love with a maiden in the tribe. The maiden returned his advances.

There was, however, a problem. The maiden was to marry a brave in the tribe and he, the brave, was not pleased with this paleface taking the favors with his lady.

One night the soldier and the maiden met in the moonlight (so the story goes) underneath the largest tree in the forest, a magnificent elm.

As the couple stood by the tree, the spurned brave took aim with his bow and arrow. The arrow went true and pierced the soldier directly through his heart and pinned him to the tree.

It is written that the maiden pulled the arrow from her lover's breast, that she then dug his grave with her own hands and laid him there covered with her fur skirt. She then covered her lover with earth, again with her own hands.

And she sat beneath the great tree and refused all food or water. On the seventh day, her body was found lying face down on the grave of her lover.

That's the legend. It may be bull feathers, but the tree is no legend. It actually existed.

It was over a hundred feet high and had a measured girth of seventeen feet.

The tree was cut down in the 1880s by Cutler Angier of Alstead. He had a carriage and sleigh-making business. Elm was his wood. Angier realized over two thousand board feet of lumber from this single tree, enough to make a lot of sleigh runners and over a hundred caskets.

For years people in the area chose to be buried in the sacred wood of the great elm of Langdon.

Oh, and incidentally, years later, in the mid-1800s, a boy found an arrowhead buried in the dirt beside the old elm. They sent the arrowhead to a museum in Boston. ❧

The Barnstead Bones

Barnstead Parade Church

BACK IN 1812 in Barnstead, a couple of farmers were at work widening the road by their fields when they dug up a skeleton.

The body had not been in the ground very long . . . at most a few months. The skull had been crushed. There was also rotted clothing and shoes. No one knew who the bones belonged to. No one in the town was missing. No strangers had been seen who were unaccounted for.

The constable was called, of course. He ordered the bones removed to the Parade Church where they were laid beneath the stairway going into the sanctuary so that anyone could look at them. They were laid there in the hope that someone might know to whom they belonged.

All summer long the bones were there with the churchgoers tromping in and out over them each Sunday. Of course all the kids in the neighborhood would look and run away to have nightmares for years to come. And people had something to talk about at the general store.

For years parents kept their children in line with stories of the bloody deed . . . the scream, the death and the ascent to heaven.

To this day no one is sure who the dead man was, but the town history tells us a year or two later a woman inquired from, and here the history says simply, "abroad." (This could mean anything from Boston to Europe.) Anyhow, some woman from "abroad" learned of the bones and of the garments found with them.

Apparently her husband had been in New Hampshire during the year the bones were dug up. Her husband, she said, had not been seen since.

This woman sent an emissary to claim the bones, and off they went. Whether or not the bones were her husband isn't known to this day, but she took care of them.

And the town went on with its business. But for years afterwards, people would still shudder as they entered the church each Sunday. ✎

Rattlesnake

BACK IN THE early days of Concord, back when the place was still called "Rumford," there was an area of the town called "Rattlesnake." Rattlesnake was over near Granite Hill and what is now Penacook Lake.

It was called Rattlesnake for obvious reasons . . . it was infested with timber rattlers.

A lot of people don't know that New Hampshire is home to rattlesnakes. That is because they have been hunted to near-extinction in the Granite State.

When I was a Boy Scout at Camp Carpenter in Londonderry back in the 1940s, the campers used to sleep out over near Lake Massabesic at the place called "Rattlesnake Hill," which, we were told back then, still had rattlers. We didn't sleep much on those campouts.

Anyhow, back in the late eighteenth century, there were thousands of rattlesnakes in Concord, and the town had a bounty on them. There were property owners in the town who actually got the cash money to pay their taxes by killing rattlesnakes, which could always be found in the place called Rattlesnake.

The Concord history tells the story of Amos Abbott who, with his cousin Reuben, killed forty-nine rattlesnakes in a single afternoon. They killed them with snake sticks—eight-foot cudgels with a hook on one end. The hook was for taking the snakes out of their den and the hammer end on the stick was for bashing them in the head.

Rattlers were slow moving. Like skunks, or porcupines, they didn't need to move fast 'cause they were forearmed.

Amos and Rubin gathered their dead snakes into a large pile that day and were putting them in sacks to take back to the town hall for their bounty when the two young men became very ill.

Apparently the collective venom of the vipers was enough so that just breathing the fumes proved dangerous. Amos and Rubin got all red-faced and swollen up. Almost died, they said.

The simple way to deal with snakes was to pasture hogs in the area where they were. Hogs were impervious to snake venom and they loved the taste of a fresh rattlesnake, as did their piglets.

I speak of how dangerous the snake venom was. It was also valuable and could be sold. Home remedies called for rubbing snake venom into rheumatic joints and stiff muscles.

Between the bounty and the hogs, over the years they have killed just about all the rattlers . . . at least in the southern part of the state.

Occasionally one is seen in the mountains.

But, like I say, there used to be thousands of rattlesnakes in Concord.

Today if someone would come across a rattlesnake in Concord, the Channel Nine News Team would be there in minutes.

Well . . . maybe not this cameraman. ❧

Concord Town House

THE FIRST NEW Hampshire Statehouse was built in 1819, but the first time the New Hampshire Legislature met in Concord was in 1778.

At that time, it was a peripatetic group holding its sessions in lots of different places. By 1789 they had about decided to permanently have their meetings in Concord, although it had not been officially voted on.

Nevertheless, a year later some fourteen prominent citizens pooled some money to construct an official hall for the legislature to meet in. The building was to be called "The Town House." When the legislature was not in session, the hall would be used for town government meetings.

Construction on The Town House was started at once, and the building was up by 1790, although it would be another six years before it was completely finished. It was located on the west side of Main Street on a rise of land set back a number of feet from the street.

It was built of wood, one story high, eighty feet long and forty feet wide. The length of the building paralleled the street. There were three windows on each side of a central door, which opened to a wide hallway. To the left and right were the chambers of the senate and house, the house being on the north side.

At the rear of the building were committee meeting rooms. A stairway led from the hall to a gallery for spectators that overlooked both halls.

On top of the structure was a cupola with a dome roof, and surmounting the dome was a weathervane built by Concord inventor Ephraim Potter. The vane itself was called after its inventor . . . people referred to it as "Old Potter."

While putting up the south wall of the hall, one of the builders, one Benjamin Rolfe, caught his finger in a mortise and injured it so badly that it had to be amputated. The man for amputations was old Doctor Carter who was famous for his surgical skill. Doc Carter was called, and he had Ben put the squashed finger on a block. Doc took a mallet and chisel and took the finger off with one blow. But it never healed properly, and Ben had pain from it for the rest of his life.

The General Court met in The Town House for almost thirty years. During that time the building was expanded but it was outgrown quickly.

And as I say, in 1819 it was replaced by a new, grand, granite Statehouse. ☙

The Year Without a Summer

Yeah, I admit the weather has been odd of late, but this is nothing compared to the year 1816 . . . that was a year without a summer.

The Warner Town History has an account of 1816 that is as graphic as any you will find.

The beginning of the year gave no indication as to what was to come. January and February were, in fact, mild. March of that year, however, made up for the mildness with temperatures well below normal and gusting winds all month. The first week of April was mild, but as the month progressed it got colder and colder.

By the first of May, after the thaw, a half-inch of ice formed on the local ponds. Buds and flowers were killed by the cold. Not one day in May was mild, and the first week in June saw a four-inch snowfall.

On the fifth of July, ice the thickness of window glass formed on the ponds in New York and all of the New England states. It melted, but the month saw a number of hard frosts.

August was no better. During the first week, ice formed on Pleasant Pond to a depth of a quarter inch.

Crops failed all up and down the east coast, from Maine to Virginia. Many had to sell their farms. Many went hungry. People took to calling the year "Eighteen Hundred and Froze to Death." Seed-corn prices rose to five dollars a bushel.

The only break in the weather that year was during the first two weeks in September when temperatures rose to seasonal highs. But the ice came back in the second half of the month and stayed through October. An early snowstorm in November dumped a foot of snow . . . enough to get the sleighs out.

But in December the snow melted, and the rest of the winter was one of the mildest on record.

Not incidentally, during the next year the first great migration west occurred. People all over New England pulled up stakes and went out to Kansas and Indiana.

Oh yeah, what caused the year without a summer?

Scientists today think it was three great volcanic eruptions in the

Far East, one in the Philippines and two in Indonesia, that spewed volcanic dust into the atmosphere and blocked the sun.

Although the east coast of the United States was hit hard, there was also extreme cold all over the northern hemisphere, including England and the rest of Europe.

And that's the story of the year without a summer, "Eighteen Hundred and Froze to Death." ❧

Deer Street Lightning

DEER STREET IN Portsmouth runs from the salt pile on Market Street, up over the hill and down and across Maplewood Avenue.

Deer Street is an old street. It is named for a public house, which was the old name for a licensed saloon. The said public house used to sit just a little bit up from the docks, and it was called the Sign of the Deer. People knew it even if they couldn't read because of the painting of a deer on the sign.

And, right where the Sheraton Hotel sits nowadays, there used to be houses. And the second house up from Deer Street was the scene of a terrible accident that has never been repeated.

In this house lived a newly married couple, the Clarks. It was June 7, 1777, and the young bride was expecting company. That afternoon there was a sudden shower, and Catherine Clark put her head out the window to view the clouds. Just then lightning struck and she was killed.

Five years later half a dozen sailors from the French fleet were killed by lightning aboard a ship that was moored in the Piscataqua River.

But, to this day, Catherine Clark is the only recorded death by lightning on land in the city of Portsmouth. ❧

The Drop Leaf Table

THIS IS A story I got from a town history booklet published by the Hebron Bicentennial Committee in 1992. The story is a reminiscence by Helen Webster about her mother. Mrs. Webster's maiden name was Hardy.

Back in the early 1800s, her family owned a fairly substantial farm in Hebron.

Now like most rural life of the time, households had very little cash money. What cash there was came from selling eggs in town sometimes. Wool fleece brought in cash money in the spring as did apples in the fall. But most commerce back then was on the barter system.

Right after they were married it seems that Mrs. Hardy wanted a drop leaf table for her home. Mr. Hardy told her it was out of the question. There was no money for such luxuries. Mr. Hardy never paid cash for anything. So that was that.

But later that year Mrs. Hardy learned that, over in Bristol, a young bride had ordered just such a drop leaf table, but had refused to take it when it arrived, due to a couple of knots in the wood which she found unsightly. The store that had ordered the table, she learned, was now offering it for sale for fifty cents.

Mrs. Hardy was beside herself with excitement. She asked her husband if they could afford it.

"Have you got fifty cents?" he asked her.

"No," she said.

He just looked at her.

Later that week Mrs. Hardy was visiting her mother-in-law and brought up the matter of the fifty-cent table.

A couple days later the older Mrs. Hardy visited the young Mrs. Hardy and told her that one of the hired hands on her farm needed a pair of trousers badly.

"If you will sew a good, usable pair of pants for me, I'll give you fifty cents in advance," the elder Mrs. Hardy told her.

And so it was that the family acquired an heirloom that passed to many generations . . . always known as the pair-of-pants table. ✦

Belling the Rat

BACK ABOUT 1930, some men were tearing down the Howe farmhouse up in Lancaster. They pulled down a wall and discovered, between the laths, a small silver bell made from a sewing thimble. The man who owned the farm and had grown up there was Joseph D. Howe and he recognized the artifact.

It was the rat bell.

See, there were a lot more rats in New Hampshire. That is, before the Industrial Revolution. Then most people farmed. Farms meant grain, corn and wheat and rye; also hens and geese and outbuildings. Those things attracted all sorts of vermin.

Well, in the summer of 1850 there was huge infestation of rats. The farming season had been very successful, and rats were everywhere. Including the Howe farm.

The rats would run in a pack back and forth in the space above the ceilings keeping everyone awake . . . not to mention how upsetting it was at meal times . . . or trying to read on a Sunday.

Now the Howes had a sixteen-year-old hired boy who lived there at the farm. His name was Millard Mead. Millard was a clever young man and a good farmer, and Joe's dad knew he was up to the assignment he was about to give him.

Y'see, it seems that Joe's father had read that if you could hang a bell around the neck of one of the rats in a pack that the noise would scare them off. Kinda like those ultrasound things they sell nowadays.

The trick, of course, would be catching a rat alive and getting the bell on it. A perfect job for young Millard. Father said, if he could bell a rat, he'd give the boy twenty-five cents! A lot of money back then.

So sure enough the resourceful Millard made a homemade "have a heart" trap and he caught the biggest rat anyone in the family had ever seen.

Mother found the old thimble and Millard made a hole in the top and put a thin wire through with a piece of melted lead for a clapper. He tried it out and it made a delightful sound. With some stronger wire he affixed the bell around the rat's neck and let it go.

"Ding-ding-ding-ding," Kind of a miniature fire engine.

Well, of course the ploy did not work. What it did do was add to the tromping sound of the rat pack a kind of fairy feeling.

Later that summer, Joe's sister got married in the house, and the wedding guests were delighted and amused at the musical accompaniment that went with the service.

For years afterwards people in Lancaster spoke of it.

Of course the music died one day as all music dies, and the incident was forgotten.

That is until the old farmhouse was torn down and someone rediscovered the bell which, for years, was kept in the family as a treasured keepsake. ❧

Railroad Accidents in Concord

THE FIRST RAILROAD came to Concord in 1842. By the 1870s, Concord was second only to Boston for the number of trains that passed through.

The first trains and tracks were pretty crude by later standards, and there were hundreds of derailments and train accidents all over the countryside. The steel in the tracks was poor, and the cars were made of wood mostly. There was, of course, no such thing as safety glass and no one gave a thought to protecting things in the cars. Also there was no warning in places where the trains crossed public highways.

The Concord history has many stories of train accidents.

On February 9, 1850, Peter Jenness of Chichester was driving his horse and sleigh toward Concord on Free Bridge Road. It was just after eleven at night, and the train of the Concord to Claremont railroad was just starting down the tracks. Jenness thought he could beat the train and whipped his horse to get over the crossing. The horse got across, but the sleigh got caught between the tracks, and the engine shredded the sleigh and Mr. Jenness with it. The history tells us that he was a respectable farmer, fifty-three years old. And he left a wife and children.

Less than six months later, William Coult and his wife were traveling in a horse and buggy at a place called Farnum's ledge about two miles north of the village. The couple came from Manchester, and both were in their early fifties.

The accident was where the road crossed the tracks on a diagonal. It was early in the morning. It was a replay of the one earlier in that the horse made it across the tracks and the buggy didn't.

The history says that the couple was returning home from a trip to New York State when they were called to another world. ❧

Roundball

ABNER DOUBLEDAY OF Cooperstown, New York, is credited with inventing the game of baseball . . . reputedly in 1839.

The fact is that Doubleday was not in Cooperstown in 1839, and never even referred to the game during his lifetime. His obituary also never mentioned the game.

Something like baseball was played as early as 1822 but, generally, it is a game that took root after the Civil War.

Before that there was the British game of Rounders. Bats for Rounders were made of three-inch pine boards carved with a jackknife.

The Gilford Town History has a wonderful explanation of a game called "Roundball" that was played locally.

It had rules much like modern baseball or softball except an out could be had by catching a ball on its first bounce and . . . and this is the most important difference . . . a runner could be out by throwing and hitting him with the handmade ball used in the game.

The Hunter boys with a friend named Stark Morrill, the town history tells us, carved the first round bats ever seen in Gilford, made not from pine, but rather willow. The boys roughed the bat out with an ax and then turned it on a lathe at the old Hunter Mill.

The homemade ball was made by cutting up an old rubber shoe and winding it with thread to make a core. Around this core they wound woolen yarn which they unraveled from old stockings and sweaters. They wound the yarn real tight . . . and as perfectly spherical as the eye could manage.

Then they looked for an old used piece of leather that they soaked in water to make it pliable. They cut the leather with a pocketknife and, using an awl with some thread from the local shoemaker (a guy named Hale Munsey), the boys sewed a perfect roundball.

Today, of course, we just go to the mall. ❧

The Old Flag

THE LOCAL MILITIA around Marlow was called the Stoddard Grenadiers.

There would be musters every year where the militia from different towns would parade and do close order drill and fire their cannon and muskets.

The guidon, that is, the colors, the flag of the Stoddard Grenadiers, was a white silk flag with five stars and two stripes. Marlow historian Elgin Jones' Aunt Rhoda Gould had hand-sewn the flag.

Well, years went by and Fort Sumter was shelled, and the Civil War was begun.

In Marlow there were few American flags. Times back then were more frugal than they are now and owning a flag was a luxury.

But young Elgin Jones in a frenzy of patriotic fervor went to the attic and took down the old militia flag and hung it outside the family home.

Well, people being what they are, soon it was nosed around Marlow that the Jones family was flying a Confederate flag. No one had yet seen a Rebel flag; of course and in fact, the flag may not have been adopted at that time. Nonetheless, it was not an American flag and so it had to be a Rebel flag.

One James Scott came over from Stoddard itching for a fight.

He had heard that the Jones boy was flying a "sessish" flag and, if no one in Marlow had the guts to tear it down, he was there to do it.

James Scott was met at the door by Mrs. Jones, who called her husband, and the couple informed the intruder from Stoddard of the history of the flag they flew.

Scott, for his part, was embarrassed and backed down, apologizing profusely.

And, as the town history tells us, the flag still waved. ✸

Devil's Gold

UNTIL THE MIDDLE of the nineteenth century, the town of Greenville used to be a part of the town of Mason and was called, in fact, Mason Village. But with the Industrial Revolution, the population soared in the northwestern corner of the village around the water power of the Souhegan River.

Trainloads of mostly Canadian-French workers came to work in the mills and formed their own town.

I personally remember a time when French, not English, was spoken in the stores on Main Street.

The mills are all closed now, turned into other businesses and senior housing. But the dams are still intact, and there is a story about a rock at the base of a particular falls.

The story comes from the Greenville bicentennial book.

Seems many years ago when the dam was first built, people believed that the devil himself had put a pot of gold inside one of the rocks down there. It is believed that when the falls were completed, there was a rainbow at some times of day created by the mist that the falls made and that this was the origin of the rumor.

No matter, over the years the rumor grew until many believed it true. So true, in fact, that one Deacon Dakin and a friend of his, a blacksmith, decided to get the treasure.

Every night for a week they snuck to the base of the falls after midnight and beat on the rock until it was broken into pieces.

The bicentennial book tells us that no gold was found. ❧

Willey Slide

THIS IS A story to make the hair on the back of your neck stand up. And it's a true story to boot. The cemetery in Intervale is where it all ended, but it began somewhere else. It began up in Crawford Notch.

The story took place way back when John Quincy Adams was president, 1826.

That summer was hot. In fact, no one could remember a summer as hot or as dry. However, in early July there had been a great downpour and several hundred feet of the road up through Crawford Notch had been washed out. There were also a number of small mudslides caused by that storm.

The road through the notch had been very busy that summer and had been busy that winter, too. That was, of course, before the railroads had been built through the notch.

But the road was there. And the road was increasingly used to carry goods from the Portland, Maine, docks up to Canada.

Those traveling through the notch had a choice of only three places to spend the night. Two were operated by the Crawford family. Abel Crawford had the Mt. Crawford House at the base of the road, and up at the top his highly esteemed son, Ethan Allen Crawford, operated his inn.

Halfway up the notch there was a third guesthouse. This establishment had been purchased just the year before by Samuel Willey Jr. who had come up from Conway.

With Sam were his wife Polly, and their five children, four girls and a boy, along with a second boy named David Nickerson. Although not formally adopted, Nickerson had been raised along with the other Willey kids.

That first winter had proved very profitable. Many people had spent the night at the Willey House, and by summer the family had made enough money to expand and improve their operation.

That summer Sam Willey hired a helper for the farm and inn. David Allen was his name. He had also come from Conway. Allen was thirty-seven and had a wife and four children. The second boy in the family, David Nickerson, incidentally, was by then twenty-one.

That first summer downpour had alarmed the Willey family. There had been a pretty good landslide from the mountain that came roaring down directly behind their house and missed their barn by only fifty feet. Sam Willey noted where the slide had come from. He built a kind of shelter out of a tipped-up farm cart and a large log he figured the family could repair to it if there was another slide. But that didn't seem likely.

But, like I say, it was hot that summer. No rain until August 28, a Monday.

Late that afternoon there was a tremendous thunderclap, and the heavens opened up. No one had seen such a downpour. It was not a rain, it was a deluge.

The Willey family huddled in their kitchen as the Saco River roared down through the notch rising by the second. At midnight the storm ceased, but the sound of the river did not. It had risen twenty-five feet and was tearing out everything in its path. It had risen so much that it was at the doorway of the Willey house itself.

Sheep and hogs on the farms all over the North Country were drowning. The crops were ruined. Buildings and homes were washed away. Abel Crawford's brand-new sawmill was washed away. There wasn't a bridge left north of Conway.

The next day, Ethan Allen Crawford led a man down through the notch. In order to do so, he had to swim the river with his horse.

When they came to the Willey place they found that a terrible mudslide had come down the mountain and had carried much of the farmland away. There were dozens of dead sheep and other animals littering the scene. But, to their surprise, the men found that the house itself was untouched.

They rushed up to find the door open. Inside was disarray; furniture and clothing were spread everywhere. Upstairs in a bedroom they found Sam Willey's glasses lying on a Bible open to the Nineteenth Psalm, "The heavens declare the glory of God and the firmament showeth His handiwork."

But of the Willeys: mother, father, five children; David Nickerson and the new hired hand; nine in all . . . not a soul was seen. All gone.

Next day searchers from all over the region descended on the farm.

The hired hand, David Allen, was the first to be found. Someone saw his hand reaching heavenward from the debris. Next to him they found Mrs. Willey's body. Sam Willey's body was found in the brook.

Next day they found the oldest and the youngest children, Sally and Eliza. David Nickerson's brother found his body later that day. But the other three children, Jeremiah, Martha and Elbridge, were never found.

The house itself had been spared because of a large boulder located at its rear. The landslide had reached the rock and divided around the home. Had the family remained inside no one would have died.

Sam Willey's brother was later to claim that Sam had visited him in a dream and told him that they had left the house because of the rising water and had gone to the shelter.

No one knows, though. The discovery of the house with all the family's belongings intact but no one alive supposedly gave rise to a figure of speech which we use to this day.

We say, "It gives me the willies." And so it does. ❧

Monadnock Lead Mine

OK, THIS IS a quiz: Where, I ask, is Mount Monadnock?

If you say it's located in Jaffrey and Dublin, and there is a whole region down in the southwest corner of New Hampshire where it can be seen from, you are right.

But did you also know that you can see Mount Monadnock from Colebrook? Well, if you come from the Colebrook area you know this is true. Monadnock is the big mountain there. But it is not the same Monadnock.

A lot of people don't know that Vermont has a Mount Monadnock, too.

And there is a legend about this northern Monadnock.

Seems that a couple hundred years ago, the Native Americans discovered a vein of lead up on the mountainside. Lead so pure that they made their own bullets from it.

The legend has it that one day an old Indian who was very sick showed up at the door of a settler in Colebrook. The family that owned the cabin was named Farwell, and Mr. Farwell took the old man in, and he and his wife nursed the man back to health.

For his part, the story goes, the old brave was grateful and on a piece of birch bark he drew a crude map of where the old Indian lead mine was. This he gave to Mr. Farwell.

The story is that Farwell spent the rest of his life trying to find the mine and that his sons, too, hunted for the location using compasses and divining rods. But to this day the mine has never been found.

Now that's the story. I read it in a pamphlet published in Lancaster back in 1938. The funny thing is, there is a similar story about a lead mine on the shoulder of Mount Monadnock down in Jaffrey.

Hummmmmm. ❧

The Dead Pig

BACK IN THE early 1800s, Keene was a sleepy town of less than a thousand people.

People didn't cage up their chickens. Lots of livestock was around, and people tolerated stray animals a lot more than they would today.

It was about this time that a family up on what is now Washington Street came out of their door to find that a two-hundred-pound pig had died in the middle of the road, right in front of their house.

What luck. Probably the hog had been run down by a horse or a wagon or killed by dogs or something. Whatever, it would make good sausage and chops. But the pig didn't have a mark on it. Now that meant that it had died of a heart attack or from something it had eaten . . . maybe even poison.

So they decided not to take the chance, but to wait for the owner to come by and claim the animal. But no one came by. And no one seemed to know where the hog had come from. And the carcass stayed in the street.

Pretty soon it was obvious that it had to be moved. And towns had just such a person to do the job . . . the hog reeve. The hog reeve appealed to the selectmen for money to do the job, and the selectmen informed him that there was no money. And so the animal just lay there.

That night the people in the house went out and dragged the carcass just far enough down the street so it was directly in front of their neighbor's house. And that night those neighbors dragged the animal further down the street to the next house . . . and so on until the carcass of this now bloating pig lay down square in the center of town, right in front of the fanciest hotel in the region . . . the Cheshire House.

An employee from the Cheshire House was dispatched to dispatch the pig. He went out with a rope which he tied around the hind leg of the animal, and he noticed a carriage pulled by two large horses there by the watering trough. Well, he looked left and he looked right, and he tied the rope to the rear axle of the carriage.

Sure enough a man and woman came out of the hotel and whipped the horses down the street pulling the dead pig without a clue that it was there. They didn't even hear the roar of laughter from the crowd watching them depart.

No one knows what finally happened to the pig, but people are pretty sure that the folks in the wagon were surprised when they arrived home. ❧

THE TOWNS

Ashland Mill

THE FIRST MILL in what is now the town of Ashland was built about 1771 on the Squam River.

The mill ground flour and was powered by a waterwheel. The two huge millstones were dragged by oxen through the woods and over trails from Durham. (There were no roads at that time.)

Many of the settlers there had also come from Durham, and they convinced their friend to come and to build a mill. The first millwright was Ensign Nathaniel Thompson who, like the millstones, came from Durham.

Back then the town was known as New Holderness. Later the "New" part of the name was dropped, and the town was called simply, "Holderness." Ensign Thompson moved his family there and built a home. Two years later, he traveled to Portsmouth to do a ship inspection. At the launching of this particular ship, a timber split and gave Ensign Thompson a nasty wound in his leg. The wound became infected and in less than a week he was dead.

The mill passed to a new owner, although Thompson's family continued to live in Ashland.

Over the years, the mill passed through many hands until it caught fire in the spring of 1903 and burned flat. It was rebuilt, as was the dam that served it.

Of all the colorful owners of the mill, a guy named "Freeman Sanborn" was one of the most notable. The town history tells us that Mr.

Sanborn owned the mill for ten years and had a sign erected by the door of the mill. The sign was a leather board with two-inch letters which read:

Since Man to Man is so Unjust,

I Know not Whom to Trust.

So I've Trusted and Trusted to my Sorrow,

So Pay Today and I'll Trust Tomorrow.

I guess I need not tell you that Freeman Sanborn was a Yankee. ❧

Atkinson Academy

*The Atkinson Academy building was built in 1803 and
is now part of the town's elementary school.*

GORGEOUS. A LOVELY Georgian structure with a bullfinch cupola.
It's the kind of thing that you look at and think, "This place must have
a lot of history." The structure, by the way, is over 200 years old.

The Atkinson Academy building in Atkinson was built in 1803.
The academy itself, however, is thirteen years older than the building. The original academy building, the history tells us, was one story,
34-by-60 feet long, and had a huge fireplace. It caught fire in 1802 and
burned to the ground.

In its time, the education offered there was right up with Phillips
Andover and Phillips Exeter. But, unlike those venerable institutions,
the Atkinson Academy always had money problems and, in the end,
that lack of money is what brought it to its end.

Nowadays the building makes up a part of the Atkinson Elementary School. It is still called Atkinson Academy.

But for over 150 years, from 1791 to 1949, this school provided a secondary education to young men and women of the area; and, yes, you heard me right, I said, "young men and women." For the Atkinson Academy was one of the first institutions in America to offer an education to both boys and girls.

It was, in fact, the second school in the country to be co-ed, the first being Leicester Academy in Leicester, Massachusetts. That academy, too, has ceased to be, and is now a part of Becker College.

But back to the inception of Atkinson Academy. It all happened like this.

In the late 18th century, three prominent men of this community decided that the young people of the area needed a place to prepare for Harvard and other colleges. A more diverse group of founders would be hard to imagine. One was a Congregational minister, another was an atheist, and the third had no church affiliation at all. All three men had high moral principals and were imbued with the egalitarianism of the great intellectual movement of the age we know as "The Enlightenment."

Of the three founders, it was the atheist, Gen. Nathaniel Peabody, who was the driving force. But he was a man who insisted his way was the only way and soon he had alienated most of his peers. The other lay person, Dr. William Cogswell, was a temperate man who kept things on an even keel. But the man most remembered for the survival, and excellence, of Atkinson Academy is the Congregational minister, Parson Stephen Peabody.

The parson, not incidentally, was married to John Adam's sister. And it was the parson who came to the rescue when the academy building that you see there was built. For Parson Peabody assumed most of the debt for the construction of the new structure. And in doing so, he put his home and land and family at risk.

Incidentally, Atkinson is named for Theodore Atkinson, the Revolutionary War hero from Portsmouth, who was a friend of Benning Wentworth. His grandson William still owned lots of land in the town. The school founders asked Squire Atkinson if he might give the lumber for the construction of the school from his woodlots in town. Atkinson was a cheapskate and, instead, gave $100 to the project. He was not well-liked.

So Parson Peabody was the driving force behind the school. It was he who saw that the school would also accept the children of people with lesser means . . . and also young women.

Up to this time, you see, there were schools for girls and schools for boys, but no co-ed institutions. It was considered unseemly. Even Atkinson had a girls' school. It was called Mrs. Colby's School for Girls. And, in fact, the original Atkinson Academy was for boys only.

But Mrs. Colby's School had closed and Parson Peabody had a daughter, Polly. So with the opening of this new building also came Polly and her friends, Elizabeth Knight, Lucy Poor and Hannah Atwood.

And from that time on, many schools would be co-ed. But this was the first in New Hampshire . . . and is the oldest continuously operating coeducational school in America. ❧

Barrington

THE TOWN OF Barrington has a fabulous history.

Many great mast trees were harvested from the woods in this town.

The town's first charter was a royal grant handed down by King George I for the part of town called the "Two Mile Streak."

Archibald Macpheadris of Portsmouth was among the grantees of this land.

In the Two Mile Streak, an iron smelting furnace was constructed back in the early 1700s. The furnace was built by a company called "The Lamprey Iron Works." Another furnace had been built earlier in Newfields. These two furnaces were, in fact, the first iron smelters ever built in America. Both furnaces were finally abandoned when the company moved north to a section of Gilmanton. That section of town is still called "Gilmanton Iron Works," and it is also famous for being where Grace Metalious lived and wrote the novel *Peyton Place*.

Barrington has a lot to recommend it.

The town has an erratic boulder called Castle Rock from which, it is said, an Indian maid once leaped to her death because she had been spurned by a lover.

There is also Stone House Pond, so-named because the base ledge on the far side of the pond looks much like a house. The base of the ledge also is called "The Devil's Kitchen."

At the bottom of Muchado Hill there was a large, vine-covered rock where a witch named Moll Ellsworth once lived with her familiar, a black cat. Moll, the town history tells us, flew away on her broomstick in a gale one night and was never seen again.

And Barrington has a huge cave called "The Devil's Den." That natural formation is eighty feet long with one chamber the size of a room and is reputed to be the largest cave in the state. ‑

Benton Buys Substitutes

IN THE NINETEENTH century, it seems everyone in Benton, New Hampshire, was a Democrat. The town went crazy for Presidents Andrew Jackson and Martin Van Buren. Even the name of the town was that of a Democrat . . . Senator Thomas Hart Benton of Missouri.

So it is no surprise that the people in Benton had mixed feelings about the Civil War. The war was a Republican venture.

Nevertheless, the long arm of the draft reached into this town just as much as any other town in America. Many of the young men were informed that they had been chosen to serve in the Army.

Now you may know that during the Civil War, young men drafted into that war did not have to serve if they could pay to get someone else to serve for them. That would, of course, cost a lot of money . . . seven hundred bucks at first. And that sum of money rose as the war progressed. Problem was that most young men in Benton did not have the kind of money it took to buy their way out.

But in Benton people considered it no shame to stay out of the war . . . they were, as I say, Democrats and their support of the war was tenuous at best.

Now, what makes this a story, is what the town decided to do. They voted to raise money to give to any citizen who was drafted and could not afford to buy his way out. They borrowed money in lieu of taxes . . . over $6,000 in fact, so that those who did not want to go would not have to go.

Benton remains, in fact, the only town in New Hampshire to raise money from taxes to buy substitutes.

There was a young man in Benton, however, who had been drafted before the town voted the money for the buy-out. The town history does not reveal his name but it does note that this young man, in desperation, chopped his own thumb off with an ax . . . this made him ineligible for the Army.

Had he but waited a week or two he would have saved his thumb . . . and a lot of kidding.

Because until the day he died, the town history tells us, this man was called by the nickname "Thumby." ❧

Brentwood

HENRY II, KING of England, was angry with Thomas à Becket, the Archbishop of Canterbury. "Will no one rid me of this meddlesome priest?" he said to his mignons.

And so it was that four of Henry's knights went to Canterbury and hacked the bishop to death. That was in 1170 just after Christmas. I bring this up just to set the time.

Seven years after the murder, a huge forest fire burned the King's Woods in a section of London. When the fire was over, some dwellings were built there where the trees no longer stood. And later a chapel was erected to the memory of Thomas à Becket who, by then, had been made a saint of the Catholic Church. The ruins of that church still stand in London.

This brings us to the New Hampshire town originally a part of Exeter once known as "Keeneborough," named after Sir Benjamin Keene who was a close buddy with Colonial Governor Benning Wentworth. But that name didn't last and the name of Keene was given to the city that today bears the name over in the western part of the state.

Back to London.

Remember the area that was called "The Burnt Wood?" Well, over the years the pronunciation of that part of London became corrupted into simply, "Brentwood." And part of Exeter soon became known after that section of London. They named that part of town "Brentwood Parish." When becoming a town in 1741, they dropped the "Parish" part, and since that time, it has been simply Brentwood.

I know there's a Congregational Church in Brentwood, but I don't think there's a St. Thomas à Becket chapel. ❧

The Old Bristol Cannon

"TIPPECANOE AND TYLER Too" was the slogan for President William Henry Harrison back in 1840. It was a glorious campaign and over in Portsmouth, the Harrison supporters got hold of an old cannon that had been captured from a British warship during the War of 1812. They fired the huge weapon during rallies in town.

Now I say, "Huge." The cannon was a full eight feet long and had a bore of five inches. That's big.

The cannon then was brought to Bristol and towed to the top of Sugar Hill where, on the day of Harrison's inauguration, it was fired to the great delight of the town.

After that, it just sat there on the hilltop until the carriage it was on rotted away. Over the years, the cannon was pushed gradually downhill until it found itself at the base.

For years, on the Fourth of July, men and boys would fill the cannon with stones and scrap metal and dirt and fire it just as it lay on the ground. That was dangerous, as the blast often moved the barrel and spewed the shot in a direction it was not intended to go.

Finally, they spiked the weapon so it could not be used again. That is, they drove a nail into the hole where the powder was lighted.

The next Fourth of July the men and boys of the town drilled another hole in the old cannon and woke the entire town at daybreak.

During the Civil War, the old relic was again towed to the top of the hill where it was fired every year until the war was over.

The last time the cannon was used was August 16, 1877, when there was a reunion in Bristol of the 12th Regiment of the New Hampshire Volunteers. That day some young men loaded the cannon with scrap and stones and shot and all sorts of stuff plus a great deal of gunpowder. This was to be the biggest cannon blast in the history of the town.

And that it was.

They used pry bars to move the cannon so it faced east. The shot was touched off and people took cover. And well they should, because the blast was unlike anything anyone had ever seen, including the old veterans. Many ducked flying shrapnel and no one was hurt.

And when the smoke cleared, nothing remained. The gun itself had been blown to smithereens.

Like the old soldiers themselves, the old gun had ended its career. ❧

Cheshire Turnpike is Free

THIS IS A story about a relative of mine, a guy named Jason Wetherbee.

Jason was a major stockholder in the corporation that constructed the old Cheshire Turnpike.

Back around the time of the American Revolution, there were few roads in the western part of New Hampshire. It was easier to get to Hartford, Connecticut, from say, Walpole, than it was to get to Portsmouth.

Road construction was hard work and, given the time and materials of the day, it was an engineering nightmare. Bridges were forever washing out. Swampy land was impossible to fill in. You had to go around rocks.

As a result, there were lots of toll roads and toll bridges and toll ferry services. If you wanted to go somewhere in early America, you paid.

People like Jason Wetherbee invested in the construction of roads and were paid back by the fees charged at the tollgates.

Toll roads were not popular. That was because in many places there were only toll roads. The local people who lived along these roads were charged time and again. And this was a time when people had little cash.

On the Cheshire Turnpike you paid your four cents, and the toll keeper would swing the pike and let you pass.

The Langdon Town History has a story about the tollgate that was located there.

The tollgate was in sight of the old Bidwell Tavern. This gate was different in that the building was built right in the middle of the highway. Horses and carriages thus passed through the building and there was a heavy wooden gate that went up and down like a portcullis on a castle.

One night, the history tells us, Jason Wetherbee was within the gate building when he heard a ruckus. It was a group of boys or a group of men disguised as boys.

They came up to the building and with their arms held the doors shut and the windows down while others in their party dismantled the gate.

Wetherbee and his gatekeeper were inside the building and could not get out.

Later they found the gate floating in the Connecticut River.

This was in 1841 and from that time on no one dared to charge tolls for traveling on the Cheshire Turnpike. All travel was from that time on, free.

And poor Jason Wetherbee lost his investment. ✎

Chesterfield

BACK BEFORE THE American Revolution, there used to be a string of townships up the Connecticut River starting at what is now Chesterfield.

These places were named simply Number One, Number Two, Number Three, Number Four, Number Five . . . well you get the idea.

As I say, Chesterfield was "Number One;" Westmoreland, Two; Walpole, Three; Charlestown, Four.

In 1752, Benning Wentworth was the Colonial governor of New Hampshire, and he was naming the towns in his province after all his friends. Number One was not to escape his attention.

In England, Philip Stanhope was the secretary of state and he was one of the few who championed the cause of the Colonies in the old country. In fact, in one of his speeches to the House of Lords, he is quoted as saying that he had "never seen a forward child mended by whipping."

Not that Benning Wentworth was on the side of the Colonies.

Nevertheless the earl was an important personage, and the governor was toadying up.

I did say House of Lords, and Philip Stanhope was a lord . . . he was the Earl of Chesterfield.

Thus, the town of Chesterfield.

And, by the way, the Earl was famous for his natty attire and most noted for his coat . . . the wonderful Chesterfield coat.

Lots of people wear 'em in this town. ✎

Civil War Riot

BACK BEFORE THE Civil War, in all of New Hampshire (in fact, maybe in all of America), there was not a town more dedicated to the abolition of slavery than Fremont.

Before it took the name Fremont, this town was called Poplin. No one seems to know where the name Poplin came from. Poplin, as you know, is the name of a fabric.

I did some research and found that poplin may have gotten its name from Avignon in France where it was first loomed. Avignon is where the French Popes resided instead of Rome, back when there was this schism in the Church. The fabric was a form of the word "Popilino" meaning Pope.

Anyhow, as I say, back before the Civil War the feelings of most of the locals were with the Abolitionists.

At that time New Hampshire Senator John Parker Hale was the leading and loudest voice against slavery in the entire federal government. And over in Exeter the anti-slavery people founded the Republican Party. Now the first person ever to run for the presidency as a Republican was an explorer and surveyor named John C. Fremont.

Well, people in Poplin admired this man so much they voted to change the name of their town to Fremont. And so it has been ever since.

So this place was a hotbed of Abolitionist feeling, but when the Civil War broke out, it was clear that not everyone in Fremont was against the Confederacy.

On the Fourth of July of 1861, Fremont held a giant rally in Liberty Square in support of the war. Liberty Square was at the junction of Sandown Road and Main Street.

The citizens cut a hundred-foot pine tree down and brought it to the square. There they erected it. At the top of the first pole they affixed a platform and a second fifty-foot pole. And at the top, 150 feet up, they hung an American flag. It was glorious.

On the Fourth of July most of the town was there to see the flag go up. There were also some newly recruited Union soldiers. The band played and, as the flag went up, a shot rang out. The town history is vague on just who fired the shot, but the bullet went through the flag.

The crowd turned into a mob.

Soon fists were flying and people were rolling around in the dust.

One of the newly recruited soldiers was getting a particularly bad beating when a man named Sandborn went in and took the lad out of the fray. That soldier, the history tells us, later died in the war.

The melee was over in a matter of minutes and the troublemakers were dispersed and the ceremony went on.

And some sort of history was made that day, although it was not the kind of notice this Republican town would have chosen.

That melee around the Liberty Pole, it turns out, was the first Civil War riot to take place in New England.

The pole, by the way, remained there in Liberty Square until 1898 when it was deemed to be unsafe and taken down. ❧

Concord Gas Company

PHOTOGRAPH BY LAURA WALKER

The Concord Gas building is just off South Main Street.

COMING INTO CONCORD from the south, no doubt you have noticed that unusual round brick building just off South Main Street. I can't tell you how many people have asked me what this building was used for.

Well, for years the building was used to store coal gas; coal gas that was made right on the site. Let me tell you the story.

On the front of the building is the date of its construction, 1888.

Before that there had been a number of gas storage structures in Concord. The first were built back before the Civil War . . . 1857, to be exact. It was a little before that time that a group of Concord businessmen decided to bring gaslight to the city.

The gas was made from soft coal that came in on the railroad. Concord, at that time, was the largest railroad center north of Boston. Two dozen trains a day came through the city. At one time 1,300 people worked at the Concord yards.

The soft coal was heated in ovens which also were fired with coal.

The ovens allowed no air to enter, and so the tars and gases were baked out of the ore. The gas was siphoned off into the tanks called "gasometers," and from there to the street lights and house lights in the downtown part of the city.

It's hard nowadays to realize how revolutionary gas lighting was. It meant that factories could stay open later in the winter and that people could go out at night. It meant instant heat for ovens so bread could be baked without waiting for the wood or coal stove to get to temperature.

The company providing this wonderful stuff had a lot of different names over the years. First it was "Concord Gas and Light." Then, when electricity came in it was simply, "Concord Gas." Then when they stopped making their own gas it was "Concord Natural Gas Company."

But back to the building. Inside the building there used to be a container, kind of a vat, made of riveted steel. It had water in it. Inside the vat there was a second container also made of riveted steel. This container was inverted. And there were two pipes that came up through the water like straws. One came from the ovens where the gas was generated. The other went out to the customers. As the gas filled the tank, it raised the inside container and the weight of the inside container provided the pressure to move the gas down the line. Simple. And it was used for half a century.

By the way, the residue from the ovens was . . . yah, you got it, the fuel called "coke." And the Concord Gas Company sold that to factories and foundries all over New England.

Later the company made not coal gas, but what was called a "cerebrated water gas," which was made from coal and a light fuel oil. This was a process that turned out much more gas in much less time. There was a residue in the tank from this process that was cleaned out each year and used for patching the roads.

For many years, the old storage building with its tank stood unused. Over the years, an oil residue collected in and around the old building. Not only did they clean up the area but in the early 1990s they were required to gut the mechanism from the inside.

Sic transit gloria.

Smithsonian Institution sent a representative up to view the building with its tank. He noted that it was history to be preserved. It was the only tank of its kind left in America.

But, alas, it was not preserved. ❧

Conway

HE WAS ELECTED to the British House of Commons when he was only twenty years old. He joined the English army and fought at the Battle of Culloden and rose to the rank of major general before he was thirty-five. He was, as you can see, a very bright and ambitious man, and he did not suffer fools.

He saw right off that the British Stamp Act was unfair to the people and businesses here in the Colonies and he understood that such actions by the Crown could only end in revolt. And he put his reputation on the line against the policies of King George III. The result was disfavor . . . although he was finally made secretary of state in the Rockingham Ministry.

At about this time in New Hampshire (and "this time" was 1765), the community of Pigwacket petitioned Governor Benning Wentworth to become an official town. Pigwacket was located in the foothills of the White Mountains in the far eastern part of the state. Wentworth was friends with the general who had defended the Colonies in Parliament and he gave his friend's name to the former town of Pigwacket. The general's name, by the way, was Henry Seamore Conway.

And the town became, of course, Conway.

Conway, in case you didn't know, includes: South Conway, North Conway, Conway Center, part of Intervale, a part of town called Redstone after the granite quarried there, and the unincorporated town of Kearsarge.

No doubt old Henry Conway would be pleased. ✒

Country Village

BACK IN THE 1760s, the Irish playwright Oliver Goldsmith wrote a poem about his childhood home. The work was a reflection of what was happening all over Europe and America at the time: Youth were migrating into cities to work in the factories. Rural towns lost most of their population as farming became more difficult.

The poem was titled "The Deserted Village." It described an idyllic country town, a place where anyone would want to live.

Now the town in New Hampshire this poem makes me think of is close to Lake Massabesic, once one of the most popular places in New England. There were places to swim and steamboats and grand hotels. All gone now. Nowadays, Massabesic is the city of Manchester's water supply. No swimming. Massabesic, by the way, is an Algonquin Indian word meaning "a place of much water."

First called the Chestnut Country because of the nut trees growing there, the township of Chester encompassed the area until the mid-1800s when Candia, Hooksett, Raymond, Chester and Derryfield, as well as this town, were carved out of it. Derryfield, of course, later became Manchester.

The town was called Chester Woods and then became "Long Meadow." But in 1845 the citizens petitioned Governor John Steele to become their own incorporated town.

Most New Hampshire villages are named for English lords or Revolutionary figures or places in England. This town took its name from Oliver Goldsmith's poem "The Deserted Village," which begins:

> Sweet Auburn! Loveliest village of the plain,
> Where health and plenty cheered the laboring swain,
> Where smiling spring its earliest visits paid,
> And parting summer's lingering blooms delayed.

So you see, the town is Auburn.
Pretty good description, I'd say. ✿

Croydon Taxpayer

ONE OF THE town of Croydon's original settlers was Captain Moses Whipple. Deacon Whipple was a hero of the Revolutionary War and was well-respected.

Well, the story goes that one of the citizens of this town refused to pay his taxes and let it be known that he would shoot dead anyone who came to collect any money from him.

That was just the kind of statement to get Deacon Whipple's attention, and he and a couple other townspeople rode out to visit the non-taxpayer.

They were met at the door by the man carrying a musket and noting that he was prepared to use it. Deacon Whipple replied that he was as prepared to die as anyone in the party, and he sprang on the man and took his weapon away from him. The men then hoisted the captive onto his horse and started for the jail in Charlestown. But the prisoner rolled out of the saddle and onto the ground. They tried to tie him to his horse but to no avail. He kept getting off.

And so the men then constructed a rude stone boat and tied the man to it. A stone boat is a kind of sled used for skidding heavy rocks out of the pastures to the stone walls. It has no wheels . . . just heavy logs on the bottom and heavy cross pieces to hold it together.

With the non-taxpaying man howling like a dog, the posse set off through the woods at a gallop with the stone boat bouncing off every stump and rock in the road.

The prisoner was holding on for dear life but he was not giving in an inch . . . until . . . until the posse got to Ox Brook in North Charlestown. There the horse was pulling the stone boat at a gallop and about to pull the poor man through the rocks and the water when he cried out.

"All right, all right!" and right on the spot he paid his taxes and costs. He was given his horse, and he came back to Croydon and was never in arrears again. And, we are told, no other property owner in Croydon refused to pay their taxes for many years thereafter.

Dublin Library

YOU PROBABLY KNOW where the oldest tax-supported public library in the world is. Right, it's in Peterborough.

It was 1833 when the town of Peterborough voted to take over and support a library that had already been established. That library had been housed in a local minister's home. That was the first time in history that a community had agreed to spend tax money on a library.

A lot of people think that Peterborough had the first free public library, but the fact is, a free public library in Dublin was established eleven years before the Peterborough library.

The Dublin library was the Juvenile Library. This library was put together in 1822 by voluntary subscription. It was mainly for the school children, but it was open to all. It lasted until 1890, when it merged with the town library.

And, by the way, there was a time when there were four public libraries in Dublin. The oldest was called The Ladies' Library, and that was founded in 1799. Then there was what was called the Union Library, then the Juvenile Library and, finally, the Dublin Public Library, which is what survives today.

So, which town has the bragging rights for the first free public library? Well, that honor goes to Dublin. But the first *tax supported*, free, public library? That's Peterborough. ✴

Dunbarton

AFTER THE FRENCH and Indian Wars, a lot of land was given out by the English Crown to people who fought against the French in Canada. The land was in lieu of payment in coin to those veterans.

Back in 1735, Massachusetts Governor John Belcher awarded land to Captain John Gorham for his valor in leading the Canada Expedition. New Hampshire, back then, was a part of Massachusetts. Thus, the governor's grant was legal. Later, when the Masonian Proprietors would claim ownership of most of the state, there would be problems with these Canada grants.

But, back then the town was called after Captain John. It was "Gorham's Town."

Thirteen years later, a bunch of Scots-Irish settlers from Northern Ireland came whose leader was a guy named Archibald Stark. At that time, the town was re-granted and was called after the leader of the group who settled there.

It was then called "Starkstown."

Archibald Stark, by the way, had a son, John, who went on to become one of the great heroes of the American Revolution. He defended Bunker Hill and later defeated General Burgoyne at Bennington. New Hampshire's license plates, in fact, carry a motto coined by General John Stark. "Live Free or Die."

Archibald Stark and the rest of the settlers, before they went to Northern Ireland, had originally come from Dumbartonshire, or Dunbartonshire, as some spelled it, on the River Clyde in Scotland. And when the town was officially chartered, they called it after the place they originally came from.

To this day, the town has been called Dunbarton.

Archibald Stark and the other Scots-Irish settlers, by the way, brought a different way of farming to the region. Different from the English model. One difference was the raising of flax and wool.

That was to become very important to the state later when General John Stark's son, Caleb, founded woolen mills at the Amoskeag Falls in Manchester. Those mills would, over the next hundred years, grow into the largest woolen manufacturing business in the world.

Also, along with General Stark, the town of Dunbarton was the home of Major Robert Rogers who lead the famous Rogers' Rangers during the French and Indian Wars.

Also Ernest Martin Hopkins was born and grew up there. Hopkins was the president of Dartmouth College from 1916 to 1945, and it is for him that the Hopkins Center on the Hanover campus is named.

A lot of history in Dunbarton. ❧

Hinsdale Post Office

The post office in Hinsdale holds a special place in postal history.

THE FIRST POSTMASTER in Hinsdale came to work on January 28, 1815. His name was Nathaniel Babbitt.

In 1815 James Madison was president. We had only officially been a country twenty-six years.

The next year the post office moved to the general store which was located in a two-story wood building on Main Street.

Over the years the town grew, and the post office grew with it. At first it was a fourth-class post office. Seventy years later in 1885, it progressed to be a third-class post office, and from that time on it required a federal nomination to become postmaster.

Warren Barrows was the first federally appointed postmaster, appointed by President Grover Cleveland, who summered in New Hampshire and later owned a home up in Tamworth.

In July of 1949, Harry Truman was president, and that was the year it became a second-class post office with a guy named Frank Young as the postmaster.

Over the years the post office was enlarged and the general store was discontinued.

A couple of times there were robberies. The post office safe was blown up in May of 1899 and again in November of 1909. Made national news.

Between 1878 and 1904 there was a second post office up in the northern part of town. And rural delivery was established in 1905 . . . horse and buggy . . . it was 1912 when the first automobile carried the mail.

So there you go. Kinda like every post office you know. Probably very like your post office in your town . . . with one exception: This post office is in Hinsdale. That's special because it is, in fact, the oldest continuously operated post office in the entire United States.

You know, you add that to the fact that New Hampshire also has the oldest floating post office in the United States as well . . . that being the Sophie C mail boat on Lake Winnipesaukee since 1892.

Well, that kinda makes us U.S. Postal Service History Central, wouldn't you say?

Makes you proud, doesn't it? ❧

The Keene Raid

HE WAS THE man who led the notorious and infamous Keene Raid back in the early days of this country.

The man's name was Captain Elisha Mack, and he lived in the town of Gilsum. In fact, Captain Mack was the man who built the first bridge over the Ashuelot River. That bridge was right where the Stone Bridge stands today. Captain Mack was a captain in the local militia and, as such, was subject to the rules of that organization.

The time was 1779. The American Revolution was happening and people had chosen up sides.

In Gilsum, virtually every citizen was a Patriot. All were for independence. But up in Keene the community was divided. Many were Patriots and espoused the cause . . . but dozens there were Tories and felt that we should retain our ties with Great Britain. Well, by 1779, enough blood had been shed to inspire zealous patriotism. And in Gilsum, Captain Mack called a meeting of his militia company at the old Partridge Tavern. It was time, he said, to clean out the stinking Tories. They knew who they were. The entire community knew their names. It was time to turn them out.

So that night he sent a bunch of his men to Keene to post guard at every known Tory household in the town. At dawn, with his sword drawn, Captain Mack rode with the rest of his men into the town, and at each house he turned out the heads of the families living there. He called them "prisoners" and had them walk as prisoners between his militia guard as they proceeded to the next Tory house . . . and the next.

Each house was searched for guns and ammunition and provisions. It was suspected and generally believed that these families were stocking up on food for the British army should they appear. No guns or provisions of importance were found in any of the homes . . . but that was beside the point. They called themselves, after all, "Tories," and that was enough.

And so it went.

All the prisoners were taken to Halls Tavern on the east side of Main Street, and there they were confined to a back room.

What Captain Mack had not done was notify any other of the militia forces in the area.

And so about three in the afternoon of that day he came out of the tavern to find that Captain Davis Howlett had arrived with a large contingent of militia with arms and ammunition, and his troops were drawn up on the opposite side of the square there in Keene. Soon after, the commander of the area militia, Colonel Alexander, arrived from Winchester.

This was outrageous. Kangaroo justice.

The colonel asked Captain Mack if he intended to keep this up.

"I do," said the captain, "at the hazard of my life!"

"OK," the commander said, "then prepare for eternity. For you shall not be permitted to take vengeance in this irregular mode on any men, even if they are Tories!"

And here his men raised their muskets.

And Captain Mack gulped and ordered his men to about face and marched them into the meetinghouse. Here they disbanded and headed for home.

As they marched silently along the road, women came out of the houses and banged on pans and pots to make a comical music and hooted and jeered at the disheartened men as they trudged back to their dwellings.

Zealous no more. ⚓

Milford-Pepperell Baseball

THINGS WERE A lot better in the old days. People were more honest and took care of each other. There was a lot less crime.

Don't you believe it.

A case in point. Lately I have been researching newspapers of a hundred years ago.

Looking through the July 26, 1906, issue of the *Milford Cabinet* newspaper, I found on the front page a story about the town baseball team playing the town team from Pepperell, Massachusetts, the Saturday before.

Pepperell and Milford had a history. Seems that fifteen years before there had been a game that was remembered very well in the granite town. That year Milford had one of its great teams. They were undefeated.

That is until Pepperell arrived. They brought with them an umpire so unfair that the game erupted into a brawl. It turned out later that a great deal of money had been bet by the umpire and members of the team.

The fix was in. The night of the game the umpire was shot with a pistol. He survived, but we don't know who pulled the trigger. We do know that he had wagered a lot of money on the game.

The paper also noted that the football team from Pepperell also had crooked officials and that sometimes members of the crowd joined in on the field to whup the players of the opposite team.

Well, it seems that Pepperell's old habits were back that summer of 1906. In fact, their manager had quit the team only the week before saying that he could do nothing with them.

So the game with Milford began at the ballpark behind the high school. There was a delay of twenty minutes before the game. The *Cabinet* speculated this was to allow the umpire and others to get their bets down.

The first batter from Pepperell fouled three times and walked to first.

On the first pitch to the second man-at-bat the guy at first tried to steal second. He was thrown out by the catcher easily six feet from the base. He was about to walk in when the umpire called him "safe" and told him to go back to second.

Well, you can imagine. The crowd exploded.

The runner knew he was out and started again for the dugout when the umpire ordered him to stay on base.

J. T. Young, the captain of the Milford team went over to the captain of the Pepperell team and asked that the umpire be taken out and a more reasonable man substituted.

The captain refused and the Pepperell team left the field and refused to go back.

The Milford team then said that they would allow the runner to stay on second if the game might continue.

There was a fifteen-dollar guarantee on the game. Pepperell would get this sum if they played or not. The captain of their team said they would continue play if they were guaranteed another fifteen dollars.

Milford refused and the game was called off. Money would be returned and no bets would be paid off that day.

The *Cabinet* wrote "as rank an exhibition of poor sportsmanship as was ever exhibited."

And, by the way, the umpire from Pepperell made no hesitation about saying that, yes, he had wagered on the game . . . heavily . . . and what of it?

The article in the *Cabinet* also noted that they hoped that in the future Milford would cut loose from Pepperell.

Ah, the good old days. Pete Rose, move over. ❧

Mont Vernon

THE ENGLISH NAVY was drinking way more than it should. Men were drunk a good deal of the time. There were fights. Sailors often fell off the rigging.

But hey, back in the eighteenth century one of the ways they paid military men was in rum. But with the discovery of the West Indies and the building of sugar plantations, there was soon a good deal more rum around than there had been before. It was, in fact, one of the commodities which ships carried for trade. But by the mid-1700s, it had all gotten out of hand.

Enter Admiral Edward Vernon, the man who broke the Spanish blockade of Portobello in the West Indies.

The admiral was a dandy. He wore a uniform made of a fabric known as grogram, a mixture of silk and wool. It was stiff, warm and formal. And because of his fancy fabric dress, his men called him Old Grogram.

It was Old Grogram, Admiral Vernon, who finally sobered up His Majesty's sailors. He did it by proclaiming that the daily rum ration given the crew would henceforth be half water. The edict worked. The men sobered up, and the cut whisky was named after its champion. They called it "grog" after Old Grogram.

Now for the New Hampshire connection.

First of all, our last Colonial governor, John Wentworth, was a close friend of Admiral Vernon. And so was George Washington's half-brother, Lawrence. Lawrence had served as an officer aboard one of the admiral's ships. To say Lawrence respected the admiral is an understatement; he worshipped him. And, in fact, when Lawrence Washington returned home to Virginia, he built an estate and named it after the admiral. He called it Mount Vernon.

When Lawrence Washington died in 1752, the estate became the property of his brother, George. And that was the first Mount Vernon anywhere.

Now there are Mount Vernons in New York, Illinois, Indiana, Ohio and Washington State, but the first town in America to name itself after its president's home is Mont Vernon, right here in New Hampshire. ❧

Peterborough Fire History

THE OLDEST FIRE truck in America dates from 1915 and is on display in the Peterborough Aquarius No.1 Fire Museum.

Peterborough was settled first in 1740, but it was 117 years before there was a fire company in town. It was, of course, a bucket brigade. That was the first method of fighting fires. The able-bodied men would dip leather buckets into the nearest stream or well, and pass the buckets up to the final man who would throw it on the fire. Even women and children and old folks would be dragooned into a line that would return the empty buckets down the line for refilling. It worked when the fire was small enough. But it didn't work worth a darn with a big blaze. Lots of buildings burned flat in the early days.

By the mid-1700s, there were two of the two-story wooden factories in Peterborough. Both caught fire . . . one in 1768 and the other in 1772. Both fires were fought with bucket brigades. Both buildings burned down completely.

But with the start of the Industrial Revolution came tub-type, hand-operated pumping engines. The town history records that by 1825, the town had two of these. One was named and owned by the "Phoenix Mill" in downtown Peterborough. The other was named "The Deluge" and was the property of the Union Factory in West Peterborough. On December 18, 1828, the Phoenix Mill caught fire. Both hand-pump engines were used in fighting the fire.

The night was so cold that the canvas hoses froze and burst. The newspaper reported that the ladies of the village repaired the hose by tying their kerchiefs around the burst hose.

The new apparatus worked. Only half of the mill burned . . . the other half was saved.

In 1855 at town meeting, there was an article to purchase a pumper for the use of the town. It lost on a vote because most people lived out of town on farms, and they didn't want to pay for a rig that would only be used in town. Let the people living in the village pay for their own fire safety, was the attitude.

Later there was a special town meeting to create just such a fire district for the downtown only. This too lost.

But at a special town meeting the next year, citizens voted to purchase a new pumper, with the people who lived downtown donating $819 toward its cost.

By August, Peterborough had its first municipal hand pumper. They called it the "Aquarius." They then organized the first town fire company; sixty-five men joined. And that was the start of the Peterborough Fire Company.

Incidentally, the "Aquarius" and the pumper from the old Phoenix Mill, and the "Deluge," still exist . . . they are in the Fire Museum, in Peterborough, located on property given by the family of Dyer Brown.

Remarkable. ☙

Pull and Be Damned Point

At the time, it was the biggest explosion in history.

THE BIGGEST MAN-MADE explosion in the history of the world happened in Portsmouth.

OK, the biggest man-made explosion in the history of the world was the hydrogen bomb blast in the South Pacific. But, there was a time when the biggest explosion ever witnessed did happen right in Portsmouth. Let me tell you the story.

The Portsmouth Naval Shipyard is where it is for good and practical reasons.

First of all, it is well-protected from direct ocean storms by Newcastle Island.

Secondly, the port is deep enough for large ships.

Thirdly, it is almost always ice-free. It is ice-free because of the tremendous currents. Only the Bay of Fundy has more rapid currents than those measured at Dover Point. At the turn of each tide, the great estuary that is Great Bay either fills or empties, and this tremendous current keeps the port open. Only one or two times in our history has the Piscataqua frozen over.

But these tides are a danger as well and for a hundred years the most dangerous place was right across from Pierce's Island where, on the Maine side of the river, there was a narrowing of the channel. This was "Pull and Be Damned Point."

Enter Teddy Roosevelt. President Roosevelt loved the Navy. He had been an assistant secretary of the Navy and he knew the importance of a fleet to a nation's image.

Teddy, when he became president, set about giving America the strongest Navy in the world. With this build-up came new technology and improvements to the national shipyards. And in Portsmouth this included getting rid of Henderson's Point to widen the harbor.

The decision was made to blow the point up with dynamite.

That spring a great coffer dam was constructed off the Kittery side of the channel. This coffer dam was a wooden box, as it were, which was built into the river. Water was then pumped out so that the steam shovels could clean out all the soil and mud atop the rock base. Fifty thousand yards of soil was removed and taken away on railroad cars over tracks especially built into the excavation.

Then the drilling began. The rock ledge projected 540 feet out into the Piscataqua River. Hundreds of holes were drilled with twenty-seven pneumatic machines. Each hole bored into the rock to a depth of thirty-five feet or more. The holes were then packed with dynamite.

The explosion was scheduled for July 22. This would be the largest man-made explosion in the history of the world. Newspaper articles speculated that such a blast might set the atmosphere afire. It might fracture eardrums. It might fling rocks into Portsmouth and break through roofs and smash windows.

All this publicity did just what you would expect it to do.

On the morning of July 22, thousands crowded the riverfront to see the big bang.

In the early afternoon there was a countdown and "KABOOM!" The greatest man-made explosion in history went off just as expected. Two hundred thousand cubic yards of rock blew 170 feet into the air and 350 feet of shallows and shoreline disappeared.

Pull and Be Damned Point was no more.

It had been blown into history. It had taken only about two seconds.

And it was all over to great applause. No one was hurt. No

property was damaged. Cleaning up the fractured rock with dredges would take another seven years to complete, but the point, the point . . . was gone.

And that, the explosion, should have been the greatest event in Portsmouth in 1905. But it was not.

For two weeks later the Japanese and the Russians would come to town to work out and sign the treaty to conclude the Russo-Japanese War. And this treaty, the Treaty of Portsmouth, would be the thing that history would remember, long after the greatest man-made explosion in the history of the world was forgotten. ✒

Moving the Raymond Meetinghouse

IN 1789 THE citizens of Raymond voted to move their meetinghouse from the place where it had been originally built to a new location that was closer to where most of the people in town now lived.

As you can imagine, it was a contentious vote. Some people didn't want to spend the money for the move. Others lived closer to where the meetinghouse was originally built. And, in fact, there were three separate town meetings and three votes before the matter was settled. Even then the vote was only 65 to 56 in favor of the move.

Those who were against the move held a special prayer meeting to impede the move. They quoted scripture to rationalize their prayers. The Old Testament tells that the Lord helped the Israelites fleeing from Pharoah, for "the wheels of their chariots came off and they drave heavily." And so did the minority pray that the movers of the meetinghouse would "drave heavily."

The day of the move arrived and the town history tells us that there were 80 pair of oxen hitched to the great building. What a sight, 160 oxen!

General Joseph Cilley of Nottingham was in charge of the move. At his direction eight teamsters stood with goads, that is, prods with iron points. At his call the animals were prodded forward and the huge building groaned as it moved about nine inches on its stringer and logs.

Three feet and chains began to snap.

New chains were hitched and the building creaked and swayed.

They moved thirty feet. Again the chains broke.

At this time those against the move were praying together, but it appears for naught.

The meetinghouse was moved thirty rods in seven hours.

And then the prayers were answered. One of the stringers snapped on the uneven ground.

The movers went to the forest to cut another stringer and they worked all night.

Next day at dawn no fewer than 120 pair of oxen arrived at the scene, teams from towns all over the southern part of New Hampshire.

And before sundown the meetinghouse was in its new location.

Apparently the positive prayers held more weight with the Lord than did the negative prayers. ❧

Swanzey

THE VIKING KING Sweyn Forkbeard was a fierce warrior, renowned and feared all over England when the Vikings conquered and subdued the population on the coast. The Viking invasion produced changes in the language and in the makeup of the population.

In Wales, the small bays on the coast were called "eyes" from the old Norse and Danish language. One town was named "Sweyn's Eye" after old King Forkbeard. Over the years the town prospered and the name evolved . . . from "Sweyn's Eye" into "Swansea."

SWANSEA.

In the eighteenth century, the Reverend Ezra Carpenter emigrated from Swansea, Wales, to Massachusetts, where he settled a town on the seacoast and named it after his native village. Thus we have Swansea, Massachusetts.

Now over in the western part of New Hampshire on the banks of the Ashuelot River back in 1733, Governor Belcher of Massachusetts chartered a small fort to bolster Forts Hinsdale and Dummer located nearby on the Connecticut River. The small fort was called "Lower Ashuelot." The fort and the surrounding area was the scene of a lot of bloodshed during the French and Indian Wars.

It was all, of course, a part of Massachusetts then. But when the border between New Hampshire and Massachusetts was established in 1741, all the northern towns in Massachusetts found themselves a part of New Hampshire.

In 1753 the citizens in lower Ashuelot petitioned Governor Benning Wentworth to become their own town.

Governor Wentworth was a drinking buddy of Governor Brenton of Rhode Island.

He was a drinking buddy because Governor Brenton also owned a summer estate in Litchfield, New Hampshire, and (and here is the important part) a second summer estate in Swansea, Massachusetts.

He told Governor Wentworth that, seeing Lower Ashuelot was now in New Hampshire, it would be nice if the Granite State (or the Granite Colony, rather) had a Swansea of their own.

"I'll drink to that," old Benning said. And that was that.

'Course nobody could spell back then. There were no dictionaries and so the folks out in Lower Ashuelot spelled the name of the place phonetically.

And so ever since, it has been Swanzey, New Hampshire. S-W-A-N-Z-E-Y. Pronounced the same as Swansea, Wales, and Swansea, Massachusetts . . . but because of the spelling of the name, it's unique.

And by the way, it is the site of the historic Coombs Covered Bridge. ◆

Thorntons Ferry

BEFORE THERE WERE bridges on the Merrimack River, people crossed on ferryboats. The first of these crossing places in New Hampshire was just south of Bedford in Merrimack. In 1729 a man named Christopher Temple created the first ferry business. The Temple Ferry was a barge pushed by poles.

Then, seven years later, another man, one Edward Lutwyche, started a competing ferry three miles south of the Temple Ferry. Now this was before New Hampshire was a state and the Temple Ferry was chartered by Middlesex County in Massachusetts, and the Lutwyche Ferry got its charter from the State of New Hampshire.

All that is important because a couple dozen years later Lutwyche sued the original Temple Ferry claiming it didn't have the proper papers. The court sided with Lutwyche and drove his competition out of business.

See Lutwyche was connected, and the whole business was pretty sordid.

But Lutwyche was to get his comeuppance. See, all his friends in high places were tied to the English Crown and he, himself, was a Tory. During the American Revolution, his neighbors marched on his home and forced him to leave and go to England. The town then took over the ferry.

Enter Matthew Thornton, the guy who signed the Declaration of Independence. Matt sees an opportunity and he petitions the General Court to take over the ferry.

Now Matthew Thornton was a hero in the state. He was a physician and a Patriot and he was known to grandstand, that is, take credit and make speeches and be seen. But people who had worked with him over the years didn't trust him. He owed everybody money and he didn't complete stuff. His neighbors, in fact, also petitioned the legislature not to allow him to take over the ferry. In their petition they said that he "never attended to matters and it was never expected he would."

But Matthew Thornton was in his sixties and he was a hero to the legislators, if not his neighbors, and the state granted him the charter.

And Matthew Thornton surprised everyone. He ran the ferry, and ran it well, for the rest of his life. He died in 1803.

The ferry ran until 1899, by which time bridges across the river in Nashua and Manchester had taken most of the traffic away from the ferries.

But the place in Merrimack still bears the name of the signer of the Declaration of Independence who in his old age did, in fact, attend to matters. That is, of course, Thorntons Ferry. ❧

The Second Vicksburg

HOOKSETT WAS ONCE called "The Second Vicksburg."

That was because both places are on a great S-curve of a river. And, like Vicksburg, there was a promontory called the "Pinnacle," where people could see for miles up and down the river. Also this is where the stagecoaches met the riverboats.

In the early nineteenth century, as many as fifteen stagecoaches arrived every day.

There were rapids and a waterfall, too, with a canal for riverboats that skirted around it, so the bargemen often stayed overnight in Hooksett.

All these travelers meant that there was money to be made in town.

In the early days Hooksett was known as a great place for liquor and there were fights and carousing nightly.

By the 1870s there were two temperance societies in town, "The Sons of Temperance" and "The Reform Club." Regularly preachers came to town and folks got religion and gave up old John Barley. Most, however, became what was termed "back-sliders" and went back to the bottle.

Regularly there were articles at town meeting to make Hooksett "dry"; that is, forbid the sale of liquor in town. The earliest of these articles dates to 1852 calling for the suppression of "drinking houses and tippling shops."

Unfortunately, town meeting day was traditionally a day to get drunk, and time after time the articles were voted down. And, in fact, at the town meeting of 1858, a motion was adopted to "find out who furnished the liquor to persons who made a disturbance at that meeting," and to "prevent the occurrence of such a situation in the future." ☙

Warner

WHEN THE LAND was granted by Governor Jonathan Belcher of Massachusetts in 1735, it was called simply "Number One." It was the first of a number of parcels given out at that time. Later, when the first settlers arrived from Amesbury, Massachusetts, they called it "New Amesbury."

It seems all the people who went there decided to change the name to reflect where they had come from. Over the years people called it variously "Jennestown" and "Waterloo." The folks who came up from Rye called it "Ryetown." But in 1774, it was officially incorporated. And Governor John Wentworth, in his wisdom, named the town after his brother-in-law, Jonathan Warner.

So this is "Warner."

Jonathan Warner, by the way, married the widow of one of Portsmouth's most prosperous citizens, Captain Archibald Macpheadris.

She, the widow, had been Sarah Wentworth. Her house exists to this day in Portsmouth. It is among the most interesting homes in the city, the Macpheadris-Warner House on Daniel Street. The house has what is reputed to be the first lightning rod in America made by Benjamin Franklin himself.

The incorporation of Warner in 1774 makes it the last New Hampshire town to be named before the American Revolution.

John Warner himself never lived there, but two governors have come from those hills: Gov. Ezekiel Straw who served in 1872, and Gov. Walter Hampton who served in 1867.

Also U.S. Senator William Chandler came from there. Chandler served New Hampshire from 1887 to 1901. And, finally, Nehemia G. Ordway, who came from Warner, went out to Dakota Territory where in 1887 he was elected governor. ✦

THE PEOPLE

Old Ads

ADVERTISING. THINK OF the number of ads you encounter in a day. Magazines, television, radio, direct mail, the Internet, newspapers, shoppers, real estate magazines, billboards, business signs, posters, point of purchase come-ons.

Might be interesting for someone to count up how many advertisements a person encounters in the course of just one day. It's got to be thousands . . . maybe hundreds of thousands even.

We think about the old days as being simpler, easier to sell stuff because there was not nearly as much competition for our attention then.

Ernest Hemmingway said that his favorite ad was a billboard in the Midwest back before prohibition. It was an ad for beer and it stated simply, "Blatz gets you drunk." Now that's cutting to the bottom line.

But the fact is that way back before television there were some clever advertisements. *The Manchester History* by L. Ashton Thorpe contains a number of ads that ran in the local papers.

Merchant Carl York wrote, "Cast your bread upon the waters and it shall return after many days! It will return in the shortest possible time and in the best condition if made from flour bought at York's Market."

One J.B. Estey advertised, "The best 50-cent corset in town for a half-a-dollar."

And J.G. Lake at 101 Hanover Street advertised, "The best one-dollar whip in town. Give me another horse," he wrote, "and put in every hand an honest whip."

Interesting concept, "an honest whip."

And speaking of ads. In the late 1800s the old Opera House had a play titled *The Black Crook* and the posters featured a line of large women, Amazons, in the play.

The Women's Christian Temperance Union in Manchester was outraged by the picture and had the mayor, Mayor Knowlton, have the official bill poster, a man named Frank Colby, put sheets of plain paper over the tightly clad legs of the beauties.

This act of hiding the lower extremities on the poster had exactly the effect you might predict . . . the play sold out! ☙

The Death of Isaac Bachelor

THIS IS A story they tell in Bethlehem. It's even in the town history.

In some ways it is a story of a simple accident. But the stuff that happened around the time of the accident has, over the years, given people reason to ponder the meaning of that event.

It happened over two hundred years ago . . . a weekday in June of 1803. Isaac Bachelor and Aaron Kenny were out at the Woodbury Farm up on the roof laying shingles.

Back then barn roofs were not boarded over. Instead, narrow boards were laid parallel to each other and the wooden shingles were nailed directly to this strapping. This way the air could circulate up under the wood shingles and dry them out. Shingles lasted a lot longer when they were laid this way.

Anyhow, Isaac and Aaron were way up there atop the barn putting on shingles when a third man arrived at the scene. The town history does not tell us what the name of this other guy was. But it does tell us that dark clouds were gathering in the west. A storm was coming. Apparently the new guy at the scene offered to help get the job done before the rain arrived. And up he went. And out on the roof.

Now here is where the eerie stuff comes in.

Just as the new guy stepped over to where the other two guys were working, there was this huge thunder clap and a lightning flash, a flash bigger than any of them had ever seen before. And at this exact moment the roof let go. The weight of the three men had been too much. As they fell, the visitor and Aaron Kenny managed to catch hold of the edge of the roof. They were left hanging there.

But Isaac Bachelor plummeted three stories onto the rocks below. He hit the ground just as there was a second clap of thunder and a second lightning flash. The two hanging men managed to get to safety and they rushed to their friend. He was still alive when they got to him, but he had sustained a concussion and broken many bones.

And here the town history tells us he had just enough time to bid "adieu" to his friends. And, the men swore, at the exact moment he breathed his last, the rain came down . . . not gently, but in torrents.

And that's it. To this day people search the life of Isaac Bachelor for meaning . . . for some sign that might have foretold his dramatic demise. What they find is simply a hard-working, unselfish, and well-loved family man with no great faults or talents.

But, like the song says, "What a way to go!" ❧

Back from the Grave

IT'S A FIGURE of speech, "Back from the grave!" but there is a story that occurred in Newmarket that gives that phrase a literal meaning as well as a figurative one.

This story happened during the great cholera epidemic of 1848. The epidemic hit this town hard. Dozens of people died.

The local physician, Doctor Kitteredge, worked day and night for three months caring for the sick. On one occasion, he had been up for three days and had just gone to bed when there was a great pounding on his front door. The doctor went to the window and called down to a woman on his doorstep.

"Oh, Doctor," the woman said. "I have all the symptoms. I am dying of cholera. Help me, please."

"Go home," Doctor Kitteredge said, "I'll be there first thing tomorrow."

And he was. But when he arrived, the woman was being taken out the front door where the hearse awaited.

At a house on Creighton Street, a woman was found dead in bed with her baby.

No one wanted to handle those who died of cholera and so only one man was sent to do the job. He had to load the corpse in the hearse, take it to the graveyard and bury it. All in an hour or two. That man in Newmarket was Charles Willey.

Mr. Willey picked up the mother and child, but at the graveyard he thought that maybe the baby was not dead, and so he put her back in the hearse and drove home. The child survived, and the Willeys adopted her.

She lived a long life.

Back from the grave . . . literally. ❧

Tale of a Bear

ONE OF CONWAY'S earliest settlers was a man named Stephen Allard.

And there are lots of stories about Stephen Allard. He was a guy who, back in the eighteenth century, faced life square on. He was always having adventures and often getting into trouble.

This story about Mr. Allard appeared first in an 1896 issue of the old *Granite Monthly Magazine*. The story was reprinted later by the Conway Historical Society in its history titled *Through the Years and Whither*. Anyhow, this is the story.

Seems one night Steve Allard was on his way home. About a mile south of Conway, just off the road to Eaton he began climbing up a steep hill. At the base of the hill was Doll of Pond.

Now near the summit of the hill that night stood a big black bear. The bear, having the advantage of a great sense of smell, knew that Steve was approaching, but Steve didn't know the bear was there. In the dark the bear stood on her hind feet and spread her paws out to welcome Mr. Allard in her friendliest ursine fashion . . . a bear hug.

Steve, for his part, never saw it coming and walked right into the embrace. He knew right off what he had done. The two, man and bear, began waltzing . . . at least it looked like waltzing.

Mr. Allard thought he was wrestling. Around they went, the bear hugging for all her might and the man whirling her around until both lost their footing and fell over.

Well, like I say, they were at the top of a very steep hill and, sure enough, down they rolled, first Steve on top and then Momma Bear on top until "Kerplop!" they landed in Doll of Pond.

And out they came, Stephen running to the right and Momma Bear running to the left.

It appears both had some 'splaining to do once they got home. ❧

General Louis Bell

HIS NAME WAS Louis Bell, and he was a hell-raiser.

But he came from an illustrious family. His dad, John Bell, had been the governor of New Hampshire back in 1828. One of his brothers was a New Hampshire Supreme Court justice and another was a U.S. senator. And a third brother was an M.D. and head of the world-famous McLean Asylum down in Brookline, Massachusetts. Another, like his father, would also become governor of the state.

But Louis . . . Louis was a hell-raiser.

After Louis graduated from Brown in the late 1850s, he came up to Charlestown, where he studied for the law in the offices of Judge Cushing.

In Charlestown he developed a reputation for derring-do and recklessness. One time he put together a trip into the hills to visit Minot's Falls in mid-winter. The party included a dozen or so young men and women from the town. It was a disaster. The sleigh that carried the entourage was smashed to bits. One of the girls fell into the freezing water, and all had to hike out with Louis leading the horse on foot. The sleigh was totaled and left to rot in the woods.

A couple years later we find him married with a wife and infant daughter, practicing law and living over in Farmington. But then the Civil War broke out, and Louis was one of the first to volunteer.

His daring and fearlessness were just what was called for in an officer. He was made a captain in the first regiment of the New Hampshire Volunteers, and within a year and a half he was a lieutenant colonel in the Fourth New Hampshire, and chief of staff to General Sherman himself.

Later he was to serve under General Butler in the Army of the Potomac.

In 1865 his unit was put aboard sailing ships and sent down the coast to South Carolina. They were to try to capture Fort Fisher . . . one of the final big battles of the war. On the way the ships ran into a gale that was so bad that the horses aboard had to be thrown into the sea to lighten the ships.

There at the battle site they dug in, tired and hungry and needing supplies and ammunition. As usual, Colonel Bell was in the front lines of the battle that day. He was no rear-action leader.

The week before Bell had been given permission to go home on leave to Farmington for a day or two to see his newborn son, but he declined because of the way it would have looked to his men.

In the battle there was a broken bridge over a ditch that lead to the fort they were attacking. The ditch was soon filled with the dead and wounded. As Colonel Bell approached the bridge, a Rebel sharpshooter took aim and hit him in the chest.

Colonel Bell called for a medic and asked if the wound would be fatal.

"Yes, it is," he was told.

"I want to see my colors on the parapet before I go," he said.

And, as if God himself had heard the request, Colonel Bell looked up to see the tattered flag flying above the fort.

"I am satisfied," he said.

That night, in his tent, he died.

The next day Secretary of War Simon Cameron arrived at Fort Fisher and conferred on the slain man the rank of brigadier general.

But this is not the end of the story.

Six months later in Farmington, General Louis Bell's small daughter came running downstairs and said to her grandmother, "Momma told me that we were to go to the cemetery, and now she is sleeping on the bed and I cannot wake her."

It was true. The gentle woman's spirit had flown to join her husband.

And from then on General Louis Bell was remembered . . . mostly on Memorial Day when the Grand Army of the Republic Post Number Three in Manchester put flowers and flags on his grave.

And the GAR post, not incidentally, is called "The Louis Bell Post." ❧

John T. Benson

HE WAS BORN in England in 1871. His parents named him John.

John's dad ran a private zoo there in Yorkshire. The boy grew up and, like his father, he too had a natural bent for dealing with animals.

He became a trainer with the Bostock Company. Bostock was the largest traveling animal show in England. And he became a performer. He went into the cages with tigers.

In 1890, the twenty-nine-year-old animal trainer came to New York, where he wrestled a lion onstage.

Ringling Brothers' Circus was impressed with the young man and hired him as a trainer and as a scout. They sent him to Africa and India, and he returned with the first gorilla ever seen in America.

About this time he also became an American citizen.

In 1910, John helped plan and organize the Franklin Park Zoo in Boston. He was then appointed the zoo's curator. This was a perfect job. Just before the outbreak of World War I, he traveled all over the world, which made Franklin Park a world-class operation.

After the war, he was hired by the largest wild-animal training organization in the Hagenbeck which was headquartered in Berlin. John became their representative here in the States.

He wrote articles for all the major magazines in America. He was in huge demand.

He also was involved with other enterprises. One of these was a health spa located in Hudson, New Hampshire. The retreat was for circus performers, a place to come and relax. It was called the Interstate Farm, and it was not a success.

The board of directors decided to bail on the project, and John suggested that they use the land for a place where wild animals might be quarantined in order to help acclimate them to the United States before they were sent to zoos or circuses.

And so it was that the little town of Hudson, New Hampshire, became world famous.

For this animal park was created for the general public.

For over fifty years, people came to Hudson to see tigers and lions and seals and elephants . . . snakes, monkeys, giraffes, and all sorts of exotic animals from all over the world.

The place even provided the animals for the Johnny Weissmuller Tarzan films in the 1930s.

The founder of this magical place was, of course, John T. Benson, and the park was "Benson's Wild Animal Farm."

John T. Benson died in 1943 but, except for a couple of years during World War II, the park remained perhaps the most popular destination in New Hampshire. It closed in 1989. With it went the memories of millions of people who visited or worked at the park.

By then it was a different world, a world John T. Benson would not have recognized. ❧

Sam Brown in Hell

THIS STORY I got from Cornelius Weygandt's wonderful book, "*The Heart of New Hampshire.*"

Seems back in the late nineteenth century, Sam Brown drove a load of wool from his hometown of Tamworth over to Kezar Falls in Maine. He then loaded his rig up with white birch lumber to take back to Tamworth.

It had been a long and arduous trip to Kezar Falls with his cart and brace of oxen, and Sam thought that he had done a good job and deserved some celebration.

So at a local watering place in Kezar Falls, Sam had a few quaffs of hard cider and later some harder stuff than that. The upshot was that the next thing Sam knew, he was waking up in the out of doors in the sunshine. But he couldn't remember who he was or where he was.

He looked around and, yes, he was in his ox cart. He looked again and realized that his oxen were gone and he was by the side of the road just outside of town with three small boys peering at him through a fence.

When the boys saw him awaken, they ducked down. But Sam saw them and he sat up and spoke. And this is what he said:

"I don't know for certain where I be . . . or who I be. But if this be Kezar Falls and I be Sam Brown then I've lost my yoke of white-faced oxen.

"And if I be Sam Brown and this be hell . . . then I've come here by oxcart." ❧

The Burnham Hanging

JOSIAH BURNHAM LIVED in Haverhill back in the late 1700s. He was what we would today call a "wheeler-dealer." He was always pulling shady deals that separated people from their money, and he was known for being less than honest.

Josiah Burnham came from a respected family. His grandfather had been a rich man. The old guy was a Harvard graduate and a clergyman down in Farmington, Connecticut.

But Josiah was the black sheep of the family and finally, in the spring of 1805, he found himself in debtors' prison in Haverhill.

There in the Haverhill jail with Josiah Burnham were two other gentlemen of the community who also were serving time for nonpayment of debts.

One was Captain Joseph Starkweather, Jr. Captain Starkweather was a hard-working and well-liked member of the community who found himself in a financial bind and unable to pay his creditors.

The third man was a guy named Russell Freeman who had been the Speaker of the New Hampshire House of Representatives and a governor's councilor at one time. Freeman had had an unfortunate turn in a business he owned and had been sued by his creditors and, being unable to come up with the cash at once, was confined to the jail.

The arrangement was informal. The men wore their own clothes and were relaxed in their relations.

Now it seemed that Josiah Burnham had been known to have had an affair with a certain woman and had been named correspondent in the divorce. This fact was brought up by Starkweather and Freeman who kidded Burnham more than they should.

Burnham broke. He pulled a knife from his pocket and slit Freeman's stomach. The poor man went down on the floor holding his guts in.

Captain Starkweather attempted to come to Freeman's rescue, but Burnham stabbed him in the side and tried to cut his throat. He then stabbed him four more times. Then he went back to Freeman and stabbed him three more times.

By this time, the jailer heard the commotion and screaming and arrived in the cell to see Burnham trying to cut his own throat. He was disarmed.

Freeman lived only two hours. Starkweather lived three.

The grand jury met in May of 1806 in Plymouth and indicted Burnham, and the trial took place at once. Burnham pleaded "not guilty." But he had no witnesses and the trial was speedy.

His very young court-appointed lawyer had never defended a murderer before. The young attorney was quoted later as saying that the only argument he could come up with was to be against capital punishment. It was, he said, the only time in his life he had ever contemplated such a position. Of course, he lost the case.

On the twelfth of August ten thousand people came to see the hanging in Haverhill. The Reverend Daniel Sutherland of Bath gave a two-hour sermon before the event. He ended his message by telling the crowd: "In a few minutes you will shudder to see a fellow creature launched into eternity! But remember that it shall be much more intolerable to fall into the hands of a living God who is angry at the wicked every day!"

And so it was. Lots of food was sold and lots of rum was drunk and some people got religion and the day was remembered for years to come as "The Burnham Hanging."

Oh, and by the way, the lawyer who could not save the man had come down from Boscawen where he had only just opened his first practice. No one paid much attention to him. His name was Daniel Webster. ✒

Characters in Gilford

THE TOWN OF Gilford has had more than its share of unique stories and characters over the years.

Back during Prohibition, the town history tells us there was a shack out in the woods off Potter Hill Road which was known simply as "The Dance Hall." This was a place for assignations and Sneaky Pete booze.

The story is that the town police chief made visits to the place but always when no one was there.

The history also tells us about a man named John Dow who was sitting in church one Sunday morning in 1809 when he was suddenly taken by some strange fit.

Poor John Dow jumped up from his pew and rushed out the door. Some of the parishioners followed him to a pond (probably Salt Marsh Pond), where he threw himself into the water and drowned. Whether he was in despair or thought he was being baptized isn't said.

Flash forward to the nineteen thirties and you'll find the story of Frank Bates which is spelled B-A-T-E-S. I say this because "Pa" Bates, as they called him, also dealt in bait, that's B-A-I-T.

Pa Bates came up from Boston and operated a water taxi out to the islands in Winnipesaukee. He was known for the straw skimmer hat he wore which he painted a different color every summer. Each spring people looked forward to what color it would be that year.

Pa had a sign that read "I have worms." One night someone wrote under the sign "Try Lydia Pinkham's." Lydia Pinkham's was a medicinal tonic sold to women for relieving cramps.

Another lakeside character was Charlie Boynton who owned a farm on Lakeshore Road.

Charlie wore a set of clothes and four sets of long woolen underwear and a long winter coat whether it was summer or winter. He also was bald as a billiard ball but wore an ill-fitting wig which was the subject of much ribaldry.

One day he was standing by the train tracks talking to the conductor, when a young man snuck up and put a fish hook in the wig and strung the line to the train where he tied it.

Poor Charlie just stood there humiliated as his wig was dragged down the tracks toward Dover. ⚭

Chewin' in Church

IT IS NOT so long ago when most workingmen in this country chewed tobacco.

So many chewed that there was not a stylish home or hotel or restaurant in America that did not have a spittoon handy any place the public gathered.

People were disgusting back then. Even within my memory, there were men who actually spit tobacco juice on the carpet in their own homes. "Good for the wool," they used to say.

I remember there was a small fire in one of the rooms in my grandfather's house on Summer Street in Milford back in the 1930s, and after the volunteer firemen had left the scene, my grandmother looked behind the door in the room and found that one of the firemen had spit tobacco on her light-colored rug. Grandmother was livid. No doubt the spitter thought nothing of it.

Up in Lebanon, the town history tells us that men would chew tobacco in church, and one Uncle Sam Crocker's "jaws kept time with his palsied hands."

Martin Dewey and Ichabod Packard chewed as much tobacco as did Uncle Sam in church, and the history says that "there were many men in those days who used to make their piles in the pew corners" and that "they were all good respectable men and none the worse for their expression of tobacco juice."

The history says it was a common necessity among hard-working men, which gave strength to the body.

Jeez, can you imagine how church smelled back then?

You'd think they'd have at least had one spittoon in each pew.

Good grief! ❧

Chorcorua

Fritz Wetherbee stands with Mt. Chocorua in the background.

CORNELIUS CAMPBELL WAS a "Roundhead," or Puritan, in England when Charles II came to power, and he was forced to emigrate.

He and his wife came to New England and went into the wilderness and built a cabin in the woods near what is now Conway. Mr. Campbell was well-read and compassionate and had a good relationship with the local Native Americans. He was, in fact, friends with the chief of the tribe, a man called Chocorua.

Now one time Chocorua was away from the region and his son, who was about ten years old, paid a visit to the Campbell's home. While there, he found a bottle which he thought was alcohol and he drank it. It was, in fact, lye, and the boy died in great pain.

On his return Chocorua was inconsolable at the loss of his son. And he vowed revenge on the Campbells. The result was that Cornelius Campbell came home one day to find his wife and children all dead and scalped there in their home.

Mr. Campbell went mad with grief and he formed a posse with

his neighbors and went looking for Chocorua. They trailed the brave to the mountain and found him near the summit. There Chocorua appeared at the edge of a cliff. He looked down at Campbell and his neighbors and said he would not yield to the white man's laws. "The Great Spirit has given me life," he said, "and a white man cannot take it."

Legend has it Campbell replied, "Then listen to the white man's thunder!" and he pulled the trigger to his musket. Chocorua fell from the cliff and landed at Campbell's feet. And with his dying breath he cursed the settlers and said that, henceforth, the land would be of no use to them.

It turned out for years cattle in the vicinity of the mountain did fall sick and die. That is until it was found that there was a great deal of natural alkali in the springs thereabout.

Oh, and legend has it that from that time on, the mountain has been called after the man who died there.

It is Mt. Chocorua. ✿

The Cocheco Mill Girls' Strike

I DON'T KNOW if you know this, but a major chapter in feminist history was written in Dover. It concerned the mills.

Some of the most available water power was at the falls on the Cocheco River in Dover. At first there was a sawmill. Later the great Cocheco Woolen Mills were built. Both mills were located there for the same reason. The manufactured products could be put directly aboard a ship on the river and transported to Portsmouth or Boston . . . or the West Indies, for that matter.

By the early part of the nineteenth century, the mills had attracted almost a thousand young women who tended the machinery . . . twelve hours a day from six thirty to six thirty . . . six days a week for forty-seven cents a day plus room and board.

It doesn't seem like much but young women were, at that time, tied to the farm and farm work was, if anything, even harder. Young women came to the cities and were able to earn some cash money in a time when most farmers did business on the barter system. There was little cash anywhere except in the cities.

The women who tended the weaving machinery were between twelve and twenty-four years old. They were strictly regulated by the owners of the mills. There were bells to start and to end each shift. The work was not physically hard but it was drudgery. It was also dirty and dangerous. Workers often lost limbs in the machinery and, if a woman's hair got caught in the machine, there was nothing anyone could do. The worker would lose her scalp.

In 1828, the factory was sold to another corporation and the new owners immediately announced a five-cent reduction in wages for the women . . . take it or leave it.

The women were outraged and called a strike.

On December 30, 1828, half the female work force turned out with banners and signs to picket the factory. The parade around the mill was half a mile long. There was a marching band and a cannon was fired now and again.

On the weekend the women met and wrote their demand to the owners. They wanted their wages restored, especially in view of the fact that the male employees not only did not suffer a wage reduction, but rather, had an increase in their pay.

The owners, for their part, laughed it off. "If you are not back in the factory by Monday, you will be fired," they said. "There are plenty of other young women to take your place." And they meant it.

And so the women returned to work at the lower wages, and the stoppage was over. And that might be the end of the story except for one fact: This was the first strike of a factory called by female workers in the entire history of the United States. ❧

Copperheads in Nashua

THE MOST PREVALENT and biggest war memorials in the towns and cities of America tend to be from the Civil War. Tiny towns have statues of Union soldiers that dwarf the other wars.

From what we are taught in school, the North was against slavery and the South was for it. That is why it comes as some surprise to learn that there were riots in New York City over the North's participation in the war, and that the Hutchinson Family Singers sang anti-slavery songs to the Union troops in New Jersey and were booed off the stage.

The fact was that many people in the South were firmly against slavery, and many in the North felt that we were overstepping in sending our young men to die in the Civil War.

Those people in the North who did not support the war were called "Copperheads," named for the snake who strikes without warning.

Copperheads were usually Democrats. Some were people who just eschewed war. Some were simply against Lincoln for his attempt to suspend habeas corpus.

As the War progressed, the sides became more and more antagonistic.

In Nashua, the Free Will Baptists' congregation split right down the middle in its support of the war. One parishioner insisted on a prayer for the Union troops and another demanded the choir sing "Dixie." The rift in the church was never healed and the church was disbanded.

After one Rebel victory, a mob formed on the south end of the bridge on Main Street to cheer the defeat of the North. The gathering incensed a jeweler named C. F. Richardson, who was working in his shop across the street. Mr. Richardson charged the mob, shooting a pistol over their heads.

Everyone ran like the dickens, and the mob was dispersed.

And the fact was, there was even a Copperhead newspaper in Nashua, "The Gazette."

The Gazette editorialized in articles against the war in every issue and even printed Confederate President Jefferson Davis' inaugural speech on its front page. And the paper got away with it. That is until one night a mob of citizens surrounded the *Gazette* office. They had come to burn the building down and to hang the editor.

But a local war hero, General Israel Hunt, owned the property, and he appeared in an upstairs window and asked the mob to disperse. It was his building, he pleaded.

The mob said OK . . . OK if: The paper would stop its support of the Confederate cause, and if the editor of the paper would hang the Stars and Stripes in front of the building.

This he did and the crowd gave three cheers for the Union . . . and dispersed.

And by the end of the war most Copperheads in Nashua had forgotten that they once supported the South. ❧

Wentworth's Last Friend

DOCTOR AMMI RUHAMAH Cutter was the best friend of New Hampshire's last Colonial governor, John Wentworth. But when the Revolution started Doctor Cutter took a stand with the Patriots and thus lost his closest friendship.

Dr. Cutter got his name from two characters in the Book of Hosea in the Bible. He and John Wentworth had been classmates at Harvard in the late 1740s. He was a prodigy and was only seventeen when he graduated from Harvard. He then came to Portsmouth where he studied medicine under Dr. Clement Jackson. He chose Portsmouth because of his friendship with John Wentworth.

In the 1760s, Dr. Cutter joined the Rangers fighting the Native Americans on the frontiers of New England. He soldiered three years but then contracted smallpox. He returned to Portsmouth where he married and started a family. He and his wife, in the end, had ten kids.

About this time his friend John Wentworth was appointed governor of the New Hampshire Colony. Dr. Cutter was one of four young men who were awarded the proprietorship of the town of Wolfeboro.

John Wentworth was arguably the most-loved governor in all the Colonies. He was fair and generous and built roads and added to the public coffers. He also built a lavish summer home in Wolfeboro. And his friend Dr. Cutter also went there as the governor's private physician. He was owner of a sawmill and his son is buried there.

So the doctor and the governor were fast friends.

But the Stamp Act hit New Hampshire, and particularly Portsmouth, hard. Portsmouth was where the money and the shipping were.

Soon there was agitation for independence. And, in fact, as all schoolchildren in the Granite State know, the Revolution began in Portsmouth, not at Lexington.

The first battle of the Revolution was the attack on Fort William and Mary at Newcastle in December of 1774. The fort was guarded by only six soldiers. So the gunpowder and cannon there would be easy pickings for the Patriots. And one night Paul Revere came galloping into Portsmouth with news that the British were headed that way to reinforce the fort. It was time to attack. So a bunch of Patriots went over and cleaned the fort out of guns and gunpowder. That ammunition was used later at the Battle of Bunker Hill. (By the way, Paul Revere had it wrong. The Brits were not on their way to reinforce the fort.)

This is just by way of saying that Portsmouth was a hotbed of Patriot activity and that Dr. Cutter was one of the big supporters. Governor Wentworth tried to get his friend back in the fold, as it were, by offering him a position as a councilor in the Colonial government. That would mean a lot of money. Dr. Cutter turned him down.

Later, when Portsmouth had blown up and the governor had retreated to a man-o-war in the harbor, he sent for his friend, Dr. Cutter, to find out how things were. It was the last time the Governor ever saw New Hampshire and the last time he was ever to see his friend as well.

Afterwards Doctor Cutter went on to be Physician General in the American Revolution. And John Wentworth became "Sir" John and the governor of Nova Scotia.

Years later, a man from Portsmouth visited Sir John in Canada, and the first question from the governor was about the health of his old friend, Dr. Cutter.

And one other note: Like Adams and Jefferson, Sir John and Dr. Cutter also died on the same day in the same year, December 8, 1820. Not the Fourth of July like the former presidents . . . but it was a week to the day of the anniversary of the attack on Fort William and Mary. ✦

The Man Who Would Be King

He took to calling himself "Lord" Timothy Dexter.

HE WAS A genuine nut.

He lived for three years in what is now the town of Fremont and for a like number of years over in Chester.

When I say he was a nut . . . well, let me give you an example or two.

When he lived in Chester, he tried to get the town to secede from the state and set up their own country . . . with him as king. In fact, he called himself the King of Chester.

He also used to hold mock funerals for himself and if his family and his servants did not cry convincingly and long enough he would beat them with a switch.

His name was Timothy Dexter. He lived during the American Revolution.

His second wife came from Exeter. She was a widow with four children. Her name was Elizabeth Frothingham and she married Timothy Dexter in 1749. The family moved to Newburyport, Massachusetts.

He took to calling himself "Lord" Timothy Dexter.

During the war, Lord Dexter got into the pirating business . . . or rather, the "privateering" business. He invested in ships that ran down British merchant ships and stole their goods.

This was perfectly legal back then. Half the loot went to the Revolutionary government and half to the sailors and their sponsors.

Lord Timothy made a fortune out of the war.

He also bought government bonds and a lot of the Continental paper currency that was printed during the war. The currency, it turned out, wasn't worth the paper it was printed on. It was worthless. To this day the expression, "not worth a Continental" means something worthless.

Lord Tim, however, bought up as much of the worthless paper money as he could.

It was a chance that paid off.

It paid off because in 1790, Alexander Hamilton came up with a plan to stem the rampant inflation in the country. To do this the country would honor the actual value of the paper money.

Now Lord Tim wasn't just rich, he was filthy rich.

But he was getting nuttier and nuttier. He took to wearing very bright and odd clothing. His neighbors shunned him and so he moved north to what was then Poplin, New Hampshire, which is now Fremont.

When his goodwill ran out there, he moved again.

While in Chester, he offered to pave Chester Street if they would rename the street Dexter Street . . . oh yah, and make him king.

No way. And so he moved back to Newburyport, where he built a huge mansion on High Street. He died at Newburyport in October of 1806 at the age of fifty-nine and he is buried there.

A very small gravestone, they tell me.

Small for a man who could have been New Hampshire's first king. ✎

Simon Drock, Colored

IN 1788, A man named Simon Drock came up from Preston, Connecticut, and paid fifteen pounds of "lawful silver money," the town history says, to purchase from a man named Isaac Tracy Jr., a parcel of land. It was in what was then the town of Newport but now is in the town of Goshen. Two years later, Simon Drock resold the land at a profit to Uriah Wilcox.

In addition to being a land speculator, Simon Drock was also a blacksmith. He was an ambitious, successful, and respected member of the community. He cleared and improved his land. He planted an orchard, including some cherry trees that continued to bear fruit well after he was gone. There was nothing unusual about Simon Drock and his family except that they were African Americans.

It isn't known what happened to Simon Drock, but there is a story about the death of his son, John. The story appeared in an issue of the *New Hampshire Spectator* in mid-August of 1825, which records "the death in Goshen of Mr. John Drock, age about 23. An intelligent and industrious colored man.

"He was attacked by typhus fever. Was attended by a regular physician and his disease wore the most favorable aspect, until a 'quack' was consulted who set aside the prescriptions of the regular physician and administered red pepper and lobelia, the consequences of which were immediately fatal.

"We understand that a red-pepper doctor from Portsmouth has commenced his operations in the environs of this town and that he has got a number of patients in a hopeful way . . . to die!

"We understand that a coat of tar and feathers is in preparation for his Quack-ship, which will probably be administered in the course of the present week . . . and that he will be able to take his departure from town in much better style than he came in . . . that is . . . on a rail!

"When will our legislature interpose its authority to protect the ignorant from themselves?"

Whether the "quack" was tarred and feathered isn't said in the town history, but I have a feeling the guy got out of town all right. ❧

Judge Dudley

I THINK, WITHOUT a doubt, the most colorful man ever to live in the town of Raymond was Judge John Dudley. Not only was he colorful, he was a genuine hero, and a brilliant man to boot—even though his grammar and syntax were often terrible.

As a young man, he had been a laborer on the farm of Daniel Gilman in Exeter. Gilman was an aristocrat and he noted that the young Mr. Dudley was uncommonly bright and able. He offered the boy the use of his library and also gave him, as it were, familiarity with the class of people who were important in the town. The boy prospered and soon was himself rich.

In 1766, John Dudley and his wife Elizabeth moved to Raymond where, among other enterprises, John had purchased a quarter interest in the town's sawmill.

When the American Revolution broke out, John Dudley put his fortune on the line in support of independence. He also was a member of the Committee of Safety, the state government during the hostilities. And, although he had no formal education at all, he was appointed a judge of the Court of Common Pleas and then a judge of the Superior Court of New Hampshire. He held this position until 1797.

During that time, he was the most-beloved justice in the state.

As I say, his grammar was terrible. The town history says he would often say "Them lawyers" and "These 'er witnesses."

Many did imitations of the judge for the entertainment of their friends. But no one ever questioned his wisdom.

Here is a direct quote of how the judge once gave a case to the jury in his courtroom:

"You have heard, gentlemen, what has been said in this case by the lawyers, the rascals!

"But, no, I will not abuse them.

"It is their business to make a good case for their clients; they are paid for it; and they have done in this case well enough.

"But you and I, gentlemen, have something else to consider.

"They talk of law.

"It is not law that we want, but justice.

"A clear head and an honest heart are worth more than all the law of the lawyers.

"There was one good thing said at the Bar.

"It was from one Shakespeare, an English player, I believe. It is good enough almost to be in the Bible.

"It is this: 'Be just and fear not.'

"That, gentlemen, is the law in this case. It is our business to do justice between the parties, not by the quirks of law out of Blackstone or Coke, books that I never read and never will, but by common sense as between man and man.

"That is our business, and the curse of God will rest upon us if we neglect, or evade, or turn aside from it."

Judge Dudley died in May of 1805. He was eighty years old.

And on his tombstone is carved:

> *This modest stone, what few carved marbles can,*
> *May truly say, here lies an honest man.*
> *Calmly he looked on either world, and here*
> *Saw nothing to regret*
> *Or there, nothing to fear.* ✺

Emancipation in Concord

OF ALL THE states in the Union, New Hampshire was, perhaps, the most against slavery of all.

This was the state that produced John Parker Hale, the first and most rabid anti-slavery person in the U.S. Senate. The pro-emancipation Hutchinson Family Singers came from New Hampshire. The Noyes Academy in Canaan was one of the first, if not the first, integrated school in America. The Republican Party was founded here in New Hampshire.

But not everyone in the Granite State was against slavery.

In the summer of 1835, the great anti-slavery lecturer, George Thompson came to Concord to preach. He came at the bequest of George Kent and his wife Lucia Anne.

Lucia Anne Kent was the president of the Concord Female Anti-Slavery Society. She would appear in church each Sunday with an African-American woman who would sit with her in the family pew.

Of course, New Hampshire had abolished slavery with the adoption of the state constitution in 1783, so the question of emancipation in this state was moot. Nevertheless there was deep prejudice in many and, perhaps, most of the citizens of the state.

The fact that an Englishman was here to preach morals to us rankled many as much as the message he brought.

A public meeting was called and a resolution was adopted which read in part: "Resolved that we behold with indignation and disgust the intrusion upon us of foreign emissaries paid by the money of open enemies to our form of government who are traversing the country assailing its institutions and distracting the quiet of the people."

Nevertheless handbills were posted around Concord inviting people to come to the courthouse at seven in the evening where the opinions and views of the Abolitionists would be explained.

Alas, the meeting never happened.

Instead, a mob descended upon the Kent household where Mr. Thompson, the speaker, was staying. Lucia Anne met the mob at the door and told them to go away, that Mr. Thompson was no longer there. Thompson and Lucia Anne's husband, Colonel William Kent, had taken off via the back door and were headed out of town.

The mob formed into a torchlight parade and went back into town singing and chanting. In front of the Statehouse they burned an effigy of Mr. Thompson, had a lot to drink, set off a fireworks display, and discharged a cannon.

It would be a dozen years before anyone from out of town would try preaching emancipation in Concord again. ❧

Guano a Guano

THE FIRST AGRICULTURAL Extension Service in the whole of the United States of America started right here in New Hampshire at the University in Durham in 1914.

But using scientific methods for agriculture go back a lot longer in the Granite State.

Benjamin Thompson, who gave the state the land in Durham where they built UNH, was a devotee of the scientific method and was, perhaps, the best farmer in the state back in the nineteenth century.

In the Hampton Falls Town History, there is a story about a man in the Hampton Falls Farmers' Club who did an agricultural experiment way back before the Civil War . . . in 1854. The farmer was one Rufus C. Sanborn and here's what the history writes about him:

"Mr. Sanborn's first experiment was with potatoes.

"He planted them on dry land, on which he had applied sixteen loads of manure plowed in.

"He put one hundred pounds of Peruvian guano into the hills, on half an acre, leaving the rest with no manure, except what was plowed in.

"He dug the potatoes in July and sold them at an average of one dollar and fifty cents a bushel.

"He got just twenty-three percent more potatoes where the guano was applied, and they were of better size.

"His crop was 100 bushels to the acre.

"The value of the guano and labor of applying was three dollars and the gain by its use about twelve-and-a-half bushels, which sold for $18.75."

And this is just a paragraph or two from the entire paper which Mr. Sanborn presented at the Rockingham County Fair in Exeter that year. The article in the town history goes on to say that:

"Mr. Sanborn is a reliable man who labors with his own hands and whose object is to make his farming profitable.

"The testimony of such a man who practices," the history says, "is worth that of two mere professors of agriculture."

Indeed. ☙

Enoch Hale's Bridge

THIS IS A story about love and lust and betrayal, greed and intolerance.

It is the story of history and transportation.

It takes place back around the time of the American Revolution.

Back then, there were very few places where one might cross the Connecticut River.

There were ferries near many of the old forts but it was slow going and ferrying a horse or wagon across the river was nigh (not to say neigh) impossible.

The first bridges were built where the river was narrow . . . usually near a falls. And the places where the water was shallow enough to ford were downstream from a falls where the water usually spread out. And even there the water got too deep in the spring and impossible when the freeze set in.

The first bridge in New Hampshire built across the Connecticut River was constructed to link Walpole, New Hampshire, with Bellows Falls, Vermont.

In 1784 a guy named Enoch Hale from Rindge got exclusive rights to build a toll bridge there.

The bridge was built of wood and went from the shore to the outcrop rocks in the river and then to the other side. The tolls were very lucrative, as this was the only direct route from Boston to Canada.

Now the builder, Enoch Hale, had a lot of money but, as with a lot of wealthy folks, he occasionally ran up against a cash-flow problem. And this one time, he went to Boston to mortgage his bridge with an Englishman who resided down there, a banker named Frederick Geyer. He knew Geyer because Geyer had a summer mansion just up the hill from the bridge.

Payments on the loan were to be made every two months and collected in Boston. But if Enoch Hale ever missed a payment date he would forfeit the bridge to Geyer.

Well, sure enough, on a day in October Enoch Hale's son arrived at the Geyer offices in Boston one day late. Geyer would not accept the son's excuse and refused the payment and from that day on the bridge was the Geyer Bridge.

Now no doubt you are wondering why the payment was late . . . and here is where we bring in love and lust.

Seems young Hale had left for Boston in plenty of time to get there before the note came due.

However, at one of the inns outside the city, he was having his evening repast when he looked across the room and seated there alone at a table was his ex-wife who had left him some years before. Whether he had had a lover or she had had a lover isn't told in the history . . . or even whether there was a lover. All we know was that she had left him some years before.

And now there they were across the room from one another.

Well, they talked and ended the evening in bliss. So much so that the poor young guy missed the stagecoach to Boston the next morning. And thus his father lost his bridge.

The history also doesn't tell us if the couple stayed together or not. One would suspect that, if nothing else, the attitude of the family probably made the encounter a one-night stand.

Ahh, the wages of sin. ❧

Ebenezer Hinsdale and the Town

The grave of Ebenezer Hinsdale

BACK IN 1704, at the start of the French and Indian War, the town of Deerfield, Massachusetts, was overrun by Native Americans. Those citizens of the town who were not killed were taken to Canada to be ransomed.

Among the captives were Mary and Mahuman Hinsdale. Two years later, their ransom being paid, the Hinsdales were aboard a sailing vessel headed for Boston. By this time, Mary was pregnant. There at sea she gave birth to a son. They named him "Ebenezer."

It was the first of many dramatic events that would occur during the baby's lifetime.

And, by the way, Ebenezer's father was captured and taken to Canada a second time, in 1709 and ransomed back again in 1712.

Nonetheless Ebenezer managed to grow up and to graduate from Harvard . . . and to become a minister. He married Abigail Williams, the daughter of the settled minister in Deerfield. Ebenezer's first posting was as a missionary to the Native Americans. He and Abigail were sent to the Connecticut River so he could be chaplain at Fort Dummer.

But by this time another war had been declared between France and England and, as usual, the Indians were again allied with the French.

What missionary work was being done with the Native Americans was with the Catholic priests.

Fort Dummer, by the way, was located near the place where today New Hampshire, Vermont and Massachusetts come together. It was the frontier.

For eight years, until 1740, Reverend Hinsdale ministered to the men at the fort. Then he resigned his position as chaplain and enlisted in the militia.

He also learned surveying and built a gristmill, the first in the area . . . and he prospered. He built a large house and a fort which he named for himself, "Fort Hinsdale."

This was the furthest outpost in the colony. About this time, the border between Massachusetts and New Hampshire was re-established, and Fort Hinsdale was no longer in Massachusetts but was now in the Granite State. But New Hampshire Governor Benning Wentworth and his council couldn't have cared less about the welfare of this fort on the outskirts of their state.

The purpose of the fort was, of course, to stem the advance of the Native Americans down the Connecticut River . . . to protect the towns in, you got it, Massachusetts.

So Ebenezer Hinsdale got very little help in the way of soldiers or money from Portsmouth.

It led to his contempt for the English administration in the Colony.

Ebenezer Hinsdale was ahead of his time. He was one of the first men to promote American independence.

But, alas, Colonel Hinsdale would not live to see the Revolution. He died thirteen years too soon, on January 6, 1763.

And although he did not live to see the birth of the United States, he did live to see his fort and the area around it become incorporated as a town and to be given his name which it bears to this day: Hinsdale, New Hampshire. ☙

Benning Jenness

STRAFFORD'S MOST DISTINGUISHED citizen is arguably, Benning W. Jenness.

What, never heard of him? Well, shame on you.

Benning Jenness built one of the first steam-operated sawmills in the state of New Hampshire, right at Bow Lake in the 1840s. And he built the Jenness Store which used to be right where the Grange Hall sits. So Benning Jenness was a capitalist and made a lot of money.

In 1845 President James Polk appointed Levi Woodbury to the Supreme Court. Woodbury had been a U.S. senator from New Hampshire. Governor John Steele then appointed Benning Jenness to fill out Woodbury's term.

In 1852 at the Democratic Convention in Baltimore, there were forty-nine ballots before a candidate was selected. Just before the final ballot, the convention allowed the New Hampshire delegation to determine a candidate. The delegation split four to four on a candidate: four votes for Benning Jenness and four votes for Franklin Pierce.

The delegation chairman broke the tie and Franklin Pierce was put up and finally won the candidacy. He, of course, went on to become our fourteenth president.

But for one vote, Strafford might have gained national attention as the home of the president.

How does it sound? President Jenness. ❧

Lafayette's Visit

THE MARQUIS DE Lafayette visited Warner on his 1825 tour of the United States. There is an account of his stop in the town's history. In that year the hero of the Revolution visited all the states in the Union at the time . . . twenty-seven in all.

On June 22, the general was given a grand reception in Concord. In the parade which was held, the Warner Light Infantry marched under the command of Captain William Carrier. On the 27th, a Monday, the general started for Vermont. One of his first stops on the way was Warner.

At the town line, a committee of townspeople met him, and Dr. Moses Long gave a speech. There was then a formal procession to Kelley's Tavern and the general was conducted to the church where a banquet table on the lawn was filled with fruits and meats and baked goods and libations. Here the general was waited upon by some young ladies of the village especially chosen for their comeliness. He didn't eat much, it was noted.

It was also noted that the old veteran looked great. He was, they said, nearly six feet tall and had a fine portly figure. His only infirmity was a slight limp due to the wound that he had received at Brandywine. After eating, Lafayette shook the hand of every person in the village.

Then he got back in his carriage. As he rode through and out of Warner, people gathered at the roadside to wave and cheer and as he passed out of sight, the old brass cannon was fired again and again. The echoes of the booming sound followed him up the valley, on his way to Bradford, his next stop. ❧

Lightning Dance

I FOUND THIS story in Peter Hoyte's *History of the Town of Wentworth*.

Seems that about six o'clock in the evening on June 26 of 1861, a terrible thunderstorm moved over the town.

There in Wentworth Village a bolt of lightning struck the home of Jason Phillips. The chimney exploded. The lightning continued its course across the ridgepole and down through the walls tearing a great gash. Dishes were broken, spoons melted and knives turned black as if they were in a fire.

And the house was full of people. A young man was thrown across the room but was able to stand up almost at once. His father was sitting with his young daughter in his lap. Both felt the shock but neither was hurt other than, the history says, a small concussion. It was as if they had received a blow to the head.

The room smelled of sulfurous smoke but no fire broke out.

Mrs. Phillips was in the bedroom holding on to the bedpost. The lightning came down the wall and leapt to the castors of the bed. From there it then zapped around the steel of her hoop skirts and leapt back to another part of the bed. The jolt burned a circle in her clothes and turned the hoop black.

Like the rest of her family she was not hurt. But she is quoted as saying that she couldn't help dancing up and down.

Indeed. ❧

E. Major, Murderer

HIS NAME WAS Elwin W. Major. He was born in the 1840s in Goffs-town and was raised in Vermont, where his family had moved when he was five.

At age nineteen, he returned to New Hampshire to Manchester to work in the mill. During the Civil War, he went to Iowa and, afterwards, came back east.

By 1870, he was in Wilton working at one of the furniture mills. It was there he met and married the daughter of a local farmer. He then took to farming.

In 1874, his wife Ida took violently sick one afternoon and was dead before nightfall.

She was buried a few days later, but the local police thought it more than strange that a woman who had not been sick before suddenly died.

It was learned that Elwin Major had recently purchased strychnine and that in former times there had been an unexplained death just before he had moved from Iowa.

There were two trials, but in the end he was found guilty.

At dawn on January 5, 1875, at the old State Prison, Elwin Major was lead to the gallows.

To the second the trap was sprung he protested his innocence. ❧

Rev. E. L. Parker Monument

THE REVEREND E. L. Parker was the minister of the Congregational church in Derry back in the 1850s.

The Congregational church still stands up in East Derry, but Parker was the shepherd to other Congregational church groups in the area and he often preached sermons at three of four different services on a Sunday. And so it was on the fourteenth of July, 1850.

He was a good man and had ministered to his flock for many years. He was at the time of this story seventy-five years old, but robust and active. He was, in fact, in the process of writing a book, *The History of Derry*.

Now on this Sunday the minister was returning to his parish in East Derry. He had delivered his third church service that afternoon. On Rockingham Road, near where the road joins the Route 28 bypass nowadays, Parker's horse stumbled, throwing the rider to the ground.

The minister sprang to his feet, but the horse could not get up. He then walked back down the road to Samuel Clark's to rouse the owner. The two men then went back to administer to the fallen horse. They struggled with the animal for awhile to no account.

Suddenly the minister rose up and fell forward. His friend Sam Clark cradled the man in his arms, and it was there that Parker died.

The History of Derry was finished by other hands and published posthumously. It is his best monument. But there is another monument . . . besides the history and besides his gravestone.

That monument can be found within sight of where the good man died.

Just off Rockingham Road is this oddity . . . a granite marker . . . with these words incised into the stone:

"Here died Rev. E. L. Parker, July 14, 1850"

However, it doesn't tell us what happened to his horse. ❧

Pickled

THERE ARE STORIES that are apocryphal that lots of people love to believe simply because they are such great stories . . . sometimes these are "urban legends." Sometimes rural legends. Sometimes surburban legends.

One such story concerns flushing baby crocodiles down the toilet. The result is that the sewer system of New York City is infested with full-grown crocs. . . . Of course, this story turns out to be a crock.

Other stories include the story of a guy, I heard, who lived in Lyndeborough who was stopped for driving drunk on Route 128 in Massachusetts.

While he was sitting in the cruiser getting written up, there was a huge accident on the other side of the meridian, and the cop left him to attend to the bigger accident.

After a while, the story goes, this guy from Lyndeborough got tired of waiting and drove home.

Next day a bunch of cops descend on his home and get him out of bed. They insist he take them to his garage . . . which he does. And when he opens the garage door, there sits a Massachusetts State Police cruiser.

Yah, right.

The latest story of this kind I have heard involves a graveyard, I was told, somewhere in the town of Alton.

Seems that back in the nineteenth century a local citizen was buried there in the manner of John Paul Jones.

Now, it is said that John Paul Jones was pickled. That is, upon his death in France, his body was placed in a lead-lined coffin filled with high-proof rum. And there he was sealed away from the air. A hundred years later, when he was taken from France and re-interred at Annapolis, his body, some say, was perfectly preserved.

Well, it seems that a citizen of Alton was inspired by this and was interred in his crypt in just such a rum-filled coffin. And there he lay, also for a hundred years.

But, the story goes, this man was not re-interred as a hero as was the father of the American Navy. No, this man was un-interred as a result of the Volstead Act. Now you may know that the Volstead Act was passed in 1922 and it made the drinking of alcohol illegal.

So a couple years go by and, sure enough, you can't keep people from drinking. Prohibition is a failure. People are buying bathtub gin and homemade grappa and moonshine and, (here comes the legend) . . . it is said that some wino-types hear about this great coffin there in Alton and they have a party in the crypt one night where they drink all the preservative around the pickled New Hampshire citizen.

Sounds to me like a Coen Brothers movie. ❧

Rogers Corner Murder

UNSOLVED MURDERS ARE always fascinating. Back in 1831, there was a highway robbery and murder in Greenfield which is to this day unsolved.

At least they think it was a murder.

The story is in the Greenfield Town History.

Seems there was a man from town, the history does not say what his name was. But it does tell us that this man had made an agreement with another man in New Boston to sell him a yoke of oxen. And this man had traveled to New Boston to seal the deal, and was on the way home when he came to Rogers Corners.

It was called Rogers Corners because a man named Mark Rogers lived with his family on a farm there at the crossroads.

Here at the farm this man stopped to buy some gingerbread from Mrs. Rogers. The gingerbread was to be a present to the man's children when he got home. As he bought the treat, this man told the Rogers family about his trip to New Boston and the fact that he was to receive some $115 for his oxen. He also told them that he had received $15 to bind the bargain. He then said goodnight and left for home. He never got there.

The theory, the history tells us, is that someone overheard his conversation and thought he had the entire $115 on his person.

Somewhere further toward town, where the road passed between two boulders, they think the man was killed and temporarily buried on the shore of Whittemore Pond.

Apparently there was talk around town and some people knew what happened, even though no one ever proved it.

I say that because The Greenfield History speculates the body was dug up and reburied in the Forest Road which was then under construction. A detail like that, I don't think was made up.

Forest Road, by the way, is now Route 31 from Bennington to Greenfield. And on that highway, near the Bennington/Greenfield town line, they say there is a ghost.

If you drive that way, roll your car window down.

They say around midnight you can smell gingerbread. ✒

The Instant Parade

The home of Alan B. Shepard in Derry

THE PRESBYTERIAN CHURCH in America began in Derry and, along with the first Scots-Irish population, came the first linen industry and the first white potato planted in North America.

Derry is the place Robert Frost wrote some of his best poetry.

And Derry is the boyhood home of astronaut Alan B. Shepard.

Alan Shepard walked on the moon and is famous for hitting a golf ball on the surface there. The ball went out of sight. You may wonder why they took golf equipment to the moon when space and weight were at such a premium. Well, it turns out Alan Shepard took only a golf ball with him. He used a strut from the lunar craft (a strut that was shaped like a golf club). Nonetheless, the golf swing is one of the great twentieth-century icons in America. What he said was, "The golf ball went on for miles and miles and miles."

But before going to the moon, Alan Shepard was the first American actually to go into space. He was launched into sub-orbital orbit by a Redstone rocket on May 5, 1961, with the entire world watching.

Incidentally, if you'd like to see a Redstone rocket, there is one on the common up in Warren, right by the meetinghouse and the school, looking ever so much like the antique it has become.

In Derry on that day their favorite son went into orbit in the Redstone rocket, people were there who had gone to school with Alan. Also, his mother and father still lived in the family home in East Derry. People were glued to their television sets, and when Alan Shepard landed safely some 350 miles down range in the Atlantic, a cheer went up in every home.

The fire whistle sounded and bells rang and people came out on the streets. Within four hours there was an instant parade. This was not planned, but somehow the citizens got floats and marching bands and veterans and Boy Scouts, antique cars, fire trucks, even the reigning Miss America was in the area and took part in the event. And right at the center were the guests of honor, Alan Shepard's mother and father as well as his sister, Polly.

A year later in June there would be a real, planned parade featuring the astronaut himself. But if you ask anyone who was around back then, their memories are of that parade that just happened.

What a day. ✒

Governor Frederick Smyth

IN 1860, ABRAHAM Lincoln gave his historic Cooper Union Speech in New York City. The speech outlined his stand against slavery and his call for a moral America. The speech was printed in all the newspapers coast to coast and was a sensation.

Right after the speech, Lincoln boarded a train for Exeter, where he came to visit his oldest son Robert, who was a student there. While in New Hampshire, he traveled to Concord where he gave his speech again at the Phoenix Hall and then to Manchester where he again spoke, this time at Smyth Hall.

Now Smyth Hall was named for Frederick Smyth, a New Hampshire merchant and banker. Smyth was a staunch Republican and supporter of Lincoln. He had also been mayor of the city and, before the end of the Civil War, would be a two-term governor of the state.

It was Frederick Smyth, himself, who would introduce Lincoln. He is famous for saying an introductory phrase that is quite trite nowadays but apparently this was the first time it was ever used.

Smyth introduced him by saying, "Ladies and gentlemen, I give you the next President of the United States . . . Abraham Lincoln!"

It was a triumph. The crowd went wild.

During the speech, Lincoln was interrupted a number of times by a local pastor, the Rev. Andrew Foss, who was a rabid emancipationist. Foss had traveled around the country denouncing slavery and calling Southerners non-Christians. He was so caustic that President Franklin Pierce himself denounced him. Called him a "disunionist."

Well, Foss was there in the audience, gad-flying Lincoln, and finally Smyth told Foss to sit down and shut up.

But Lincoln is quoted as saying, "Let the gentleman ask his questions, and I will answer them."

Reverend Foss is buried in the Valley Cemetery in Manchester . . . Smyth would go down in state history as being one of the best governors. He managed to rescue the state from bankruptcy after the Civil War, and he presided over the creation of the school that would later become the University of New Hampshire.

He died in 1899. ●

Dottie Sparks

IT WAS THE summer of 1942. Pearl Harbor had happened only seven months before. In July, a 21-year-old woman named Dottie Sparks came up from Media, Pennsylvania, to spend a few days in Conway.

On this particular day, she and some friends were over in Passaconaway at Rocky Gorge on the Swift River bathing and picnicking and lying out in the sun. Later in the afternoon, the group was packing up their things when they discovered that Dottie was not there.

Soon the area was crawling with volunteers calling out the young woman's name and searching the woods. People from Public Service and cops and Boy Scouts were there, and even the local undertaker was there with his hearse, and the medical examiner.

Someone saw something pink under the waterfall. Dottie had been wearing a pink bathing suit. The men went upstream from the waterfall to dam up the stream so that they could get at the body. It didn't work.

Otis Johnson stood at the top of the falls with a grappling hook. He got hold of the swimsuit but couldn't pull the woman up.

Chick Whitcomb was there. He had been fishing just downstream from the falls.

So was Kenneth Haywood. Ken was big and powerful. He would later become a New Hampshire State Trooper.

Anyhow, Ken took Chick Whitcomb by the ankles and dangled him down through the waterfall.

Otis Johnson had managed to pull the woman up a little and Chick reached out and caught her by the wrists.

And his blood ran cold.

As he pulled the wrists, the young woman also closed her hands around his wrists. She was alive!

Problem was that her ankle was caught in between a couple rocks at the base of the falls. It took a number of minutes but Chick managed to free her and get her to dry land.

It had been over three hours, but Dottie had managed to keep her head down and was able to breathe. But she could not call out.

They took her to the doctor and then to bed, and she recovered within a day or so. And she went on to serve in the U.S. Army as a WAC in World War II. ❧

The Beer Bottle Spire

PHOTOGRAPHS BY LAURA WALKER

Regarding the spire in Hampton Falls, it is not what some think.

FACING THE TOWN common, in the town of Hampton Falls, there sits a white church with a thin spire that can be seen for miles. This is the First Baptist Church.

On any day you may see people on the common taking pictures of the acanthus leaf finial at the apex of the steeple. People come from miles around to see and photograph this finial. This is because at the very top of the finial there appears to be a beer bottle . . . yes, a beer bottle, pointing the way to heaven for the Hampton Falls Baptists.

I have been told that the bottle was a gift from Portsmouth brewer Frank Jones back around the Civil War. Jones was the richest man in the area back then and what he said, went. And if he said he wanted a model of his ale bottle on top of the church then you bet it would be there.

Of course, all this is nonsense. Although Frank Jones was a Baptist and financed the renovation of the Middle Street Baptist Church in Portsmouth in the 1890s, alas, he gave no money to the Hampton Falls church.

The steeple and the finial were financed by the Dodge family. The Dodge family, and specifically Betsey Fifield Dodge, invited the first Baptist preachers to her home in Hampton Falls in 1816.

The Baptist Meetinghouse was built in 1836. It had no steeple. Twenty-three years later the church was fancied up with a grand spire and a slate roof and frescos and a carpet. It was then that the finial with its bottle-like apex was affixed to the steeple. It is not meant to be a bottle.

It is simply a common design of the time.

By the way, an earthquake occurred in Hampton Falls about ten years before the church was built. At that time, the smell of sulphur permeated the air around the common. From then on, the place was called "Brimstone Hill."

But, these are Baptists, so this is certainly not a place of "fire and brimstone."

Nor is the church's symbol a beer bottle. ✒

Spiritualism in New Hampshire

RIGHT AFTER THE Civil War, there was tremendous interest in Spiritualism. People wanted to get in touch with soldiers who had died in the conflict.

Mary Todd Lincoln employed a Spiritualist in the White House to contact her dead sons, Eddie and Willie and later her dead husband. There is a noted photograph of her with a spirit image of Abe standing behind her.

Even Queen Victoria used Spiritualists to contact her dead husband, Albert.

New Hampshire also had Spiritualists.

In Rindge in 1885, Spiritualists purchased property on Long Pond and built a park there. They called it "The Mediumistic Camp Meeting of the Two Worlds." The "Two Worlds" were this world and the spiritual world.

This was a new thing then. See, the first practitioners of Spiritualism were generally liberals . . . Unitarians and Universalists and the like . . . and their gatherings were more like lectures or Chautauquas. Speakers would discuss the idea in rational terms.

But after the Civil War, the Baptists and Methodists embraced Spiritualism, and they brought the tradition of camp meetings to the belief.

Incidentally, Spiritualists generally saw no conflict between holding seances and attending regular church. Most people who believed in Spiritualism did not see it as a separate religion, although some did.

In Jaffrey, the Spiritualists renamed Long Pond. They called it "Sunshine Lake." In fact, when I was a teenager, most people with cottages on the lake still called it "Sunshine Lake."

The campground was located on the southeastern shore of the lake. There they built a tabernacle with stained glass that could accommodate 500 people. Building lots were laid out for the faithful to purchase and over three dozen did just that.

On the lake the camp had its own steam-powered launch which went from the camp to the public beach at the Jaffrey side.

No alcohol was allowed at the facility and the followers were encouraged always to be conservative. Not all the Spiritualists were conservative. In the state of New York, in fact, some Spiritualists practiced free love. But on Sunshine Lake there was never any hanky panky.

The park they built was called Woodmere, and the section of town where it was is called that to this day.

The Spiritualists prospered until about 1890 when membership in the faith dropped off considerably. Very few young people came to the practice and, by the turn of the century, it was all over.

In 1911, Hiram Clark sold the remaining lots of the once-thriving community. Hiram was the only Spiritualist from town. Most of the others had come from Massachusetts.

The townsfolk generally did not like the fact that the Spiritualists were there. In fact, in 1911, Senator Charles Rich of Jaffrey got the legislature to officially change the name of the lake to Contoocook.

Lake Sunshine was the invention of the Spiritualists and they wanted no trace of them left. That was the end of Spiritualism in Rindge. ☙

The Stolen Mittens

MARY ROWELL WAS a pretty girl. She had raven black hair and very pale skin and red cheeks. She was seventeen years old.

In 1854, she was working as a maid in the service of Mrs. Lois Sholes in Goshen. Well, Mrs. Sholes had a tea party one afternoon and Mary Rowell served, and after the party one of the women left without, she said, her new black silk mittens.

Now silk mittens were all the rage in 1854.

What it all came down to was that the mittens were missing and the only explanation was that Mary Rowell had taken them. Her room was searched, and nothing was found.

She was never seen wearing black mittens. Someone said, however, that they saw black silk threads entangled in the rose bush beneath Mary's window. There were especially two unnamed women in town who believed that Mary was a thief.

Well, some weeks went by and one night Mary had a toothache.

Her employer, Lois Sholes, gave her the standard toothache medicine, cloves and whisky and sent her to bed. Later, before dawn, Mrs. Sholes went up the stairs to check on Mary and found her room empty. She called and got no answer. It was then she noted that the door to the attic stairway was open.

At the top of the stairs she found her . . . dangling from the rafters. Mary Rowell had hanged herself with a scarf she herself had knitted.

Mary's tombstone in the North Cemetery reads:

> *Dearly beloved while on earth*
> *Deeply lamented in death*
> *Borne down by two cruel oppressors*
> *Distracted and dead.*

To this day no one knows what happened to the mittens. Nor do we know who the "two cruel oppressors" were. ❧

The Thief Barber

HERE IS ANOTHER story from Charles Brewster's great book, *Rambles About Portsmouth*, published back in 1859. It's a story about a lie detector.

Of course the lie detector is a modern invention. It works by measuring heartbeat and blood pressure and the amount of electricity and sweat that a person exudes when confronted with a question that they don't wish to deal with.

Well, this is a story about the same thing.

It happened in Portsmouth about the time of the Revolutionary War. At that time, there was a barbershop in the row where the Portsmouth Atheneum (the oldest private library in the area) now sits. The shop was owned by a man named Peter Mann, and he had an apprentice, a dashing and handsome young feller named Sam Chandler.

Now at the time our story takes place there had been a series of burglaries in town. Sometime during the year, someone had snuck into Mr. Cutts' Dry Goods Store and made off with tools and clothing and kitchenware. Mr. Griffith, the jeweler, had been robbed of a couple watches. The town was talking of nothing else . . . especially at the barber shop where gossip was stock and trade.

Now on a day in January, George Dame came into the shop for his usual shave, and he said to the owner, Mr. Mann, "Peter," he said, "so you've been stealing more goods."

It was a joke, and Peter laughed out loud.

And then, as he sat in the chair to be shaved, George Dame turned to young Sam and said, in mock seriousness, "Tell me, Sam, what did you do with the goods?"

Well, Sam Chandler went to shave George but his hand was not steady. In fact, he shook so much that George asked the other barber to shave him.

And so it was that Sam Chandler was arrested. He later confessed and lead authorities to the attic of the old statehouse where he had hidden his cache of loot which he had amassed over the year. He stole the stuff, he said, because he intended to start his own store somewhere and didn't have money or credit to get started.

Perhaps the most surprising thing about this case is that young Chandler was not jailed or fined. Instead he was banished from Portsmouth forever.

So, if he ever did open a store, it certainly was somewhere else. ❧

The Ugly Murderer

UP IN PLAINFIELD, back in 1896, there was a guy named Walter H. Hunt.

Hunt was thirty years old and he was a mean man. He was known to get drunk and attack his wife with a knife. More than once the poor woman sought refuge with a neighbor when her husband went on a toot. Everybody in town knew the man was dangerous and crazy.

Well, Walter H. Hunt took a dislike especially to a 20-year-old lad from down the road, a guy named Irving Smith. Seems Walter's wife had said that Smith was cute and had lovely black curls. It was, apparently, her way of torturing her husband. Great fun.

Except for poor Irving Smith.

One morning Smith was digging potatoes down on the Levi Nelson farm when Walter Hunt showed up. The upshot (and "shot" is the operative word here) was that Smith was plugged in the stomach, the back and the back of the head. The shots were fired so close that they set the victim's clothes on fire.

Beside the body Hunt threw his empty whisky bottle. Then he ran into the woods. The word got out and men from all over Plainfield, as well as Cornish and Lebanon, converged on the site. A posse formed and the woods surrounded. The searchers beat the bush, and soon Hunt was found. He was beside Blow Me Down Brook, and he had shot himself to death.

Unspeakable crime and justice all within a few hours.

But the last word that day was from a prominent unidentified man who is quoted in the town history as saying, "Walter H. Hunt had the meanest shaped head I have ever seen on a human being."

But, like they say, "Handsome is as handsome does." ✒

Daniel on Horseback

BACK IN 1840, Daniel Webster was traveling from Keene to Nashua by horseback. As he came through Peterborough, he was recognized and agreed to make a few remarks at Colonel French's Tavern in that town. After the gathering the great orator shook hands and went on his way.

Coming through the town of Temple, Daniel Webster's horse began to falter and he had to walk beside the animal. As he came down the road, he met a resident of the town, an older man who introduced himself as a Mr. Boynton. Mr. Boynton was riding a spirited horse, and Daniel Webster asked if he might ride the better horse to Wilton where he would procure another horse for the rest of the ride to Nashua. Webster said that he would pay the man.

Mr. Boynton had nothing better to do, and so invited Webster to mount up behind him on his horse and, with the lame horse walking behind, the two men rode on to the next town.

During the ride, the older man engaged his fellow rider in a conversation about politics and the federal government and, quite naturally, Daniel Webster's name came up.

"Did you ever see Daniel Webster, Mr. Boynton?"

"Yes, I saw him once in Portsmouth many years ago."

"Do you think you'd recognize him if you ever saw him again?"

"Yes, I think I might."

And here Daniel Webster raised his hat and, with his face only inches from Mr. Boynton's face, he said, "Did you ever see me before?"

Mr. Boynton drew his head back and looked at him.

"I declare," he said. "I believe you are the very critter."

And the two men laughed heartily as the horse continued his way to Wilton. ❧

Wentworth's Revenge

THE WENTWORTH COOLIDGE Mansion on Little Harbor in Portsmouth is the home where New Hampshire's Colonial Governor Benning Wentworth lived back before the American Revolution.

It was there that old Benning married the scullery maid, one Martha Hilton, when he was sixty and she only twenty . . . the old goat.

Benning Wentworth was the richest man in Portsmouth in his time. That was because he was connected. He knew all the important personages in the British Admiralty and all the important men in government there. That allowed him to build ships and to trade with the Continent and the West Indies. Benning Wentworth made his fortune trading lumber and rum and slaves.

He was also ruthless. Here's an example: Seems the governor could buy about anything, but he could not buy fate. And his three sons and his wife all died before he was fifty-eight. In his old age the governor then decided to take a new wife. Now this was before he became smitten with the kitchen help.

See, at first, he wanted a woman of his own rank. Such a woman was Molly Pitman. She was all honey and curls and blue eyes and the governor was sure his wealth would overcome any hesitation the lady might have about his age and girth.

But, alas, Molly was in love with another . . . a lowly mechanic named Richard Shortridge . . . and so she turned old Benning down flat. What a humiliation. Especially when later she married Shortridge.

But the governor would have his revenge. Seems there was a British frigate at anchor in Portsmouth Harbor. So old Benning paid the captain to have some men from his ship go ashore to the home of the couple and kidnap the bridegroom and press him into service aboard ship. It was a full seven years before poor Richard Shortridge got back to Portsmouth and his beloved Molly.

She, for her part, remained steadfast and faithful, and over the years the couple had many children.

And, like I say, old Benning married the maid. ❧

First Murder in Hillsborough County

THE FIRST MAN to be tried for murder in Hillsborough County was a man from Hollis.

Since it was the first murder trial, it was historically important. But equally important was the defendant's plea to the charge, a plea which is, to this day, unique in New Hampshire jurisprudence.

The indicted man was Israel Wilkins, Jr. In September of 1733, a grand jury charged him with the murder of his father, Israel Wilkins, Sr.

The crime was the result of an argument. According to the charges brought by the grand jury, the deceased was mortally wounded by "a blow upon the head with a certain billet of wood." The defendant, the charges said, "thereby gave the deceased upon his left temple, a mortal wound of the length of three inches and the depth of one inch of which," it goes on to say, "the said deceased, after languishing for the space of three days, then and there died."

A jury in Amherst found Israel Wilkins, Jr. guilty of manslaughter. Manslaughter was, in 1733, punishable by death, the same as premeditated murder. At the sentencing, the judge asked the prisoner if he knew of any reason the sentence of death should not be passed upon him, and Israel Wilkins, Jr. then prayed "the benefit of clergy," which was granted.

This was the first and last time in the history of New Hampshire law that anyone asked for or received this favor, this thing called benefit of clergy. And, in fact, sixty years later the U.S. Congress would pass a law making benefit of clergy illegal.

Now benefit of clergy was an English law which allowed members of the clergy to be tried, not by a secular court, but rather by their peers, that is, other clergymen. These juries seldom gave the death penalty. Later the law was expanded to people who could prove they could read and write. These were not thought to be criminal types.

Still later, benefit of clergy was granted anyone who had never before committed a crime and this was the basis for Israel Wilkins' plea. The plea was granted and the prisoner was not killed, rather the letter "T" was branded with a hot iron on his left thumb, and all his property was confiscated by the state.

I'm not sure what the letter "T" stood for. ❧

Worky

I OWE THIS story to Ray Brighton, the Portsmouth historian whom I knew quite well. He died a while ago and I miss him. I would call him on occasion when I was stuck about some piece of Portsmouth history. He always knew the answer. He never disappointed me.

Ray tells this story about Harrison Workman who was known locally as "Worky."

Worky had been in the U.S. Army during World War II. He had worked in Portsmouth Harbor as a mine planter. After the war, Worky had gone back to lobstering.

Well, one morning he was at the pier alone in his boat pulling in his lines when he found himself face to face with a dead man. Someone had fallen in the water and drowned and had become entangled in the lines.

So Worky walked into town and called the police and went back to the boat to wait for them to come and, as he had done during the war when there was a respite from work, he lay down on the dock to take a nap 'til they got there.

Well, you guessed it; Worky woke up to find someone under his arms and another lifting his legs to put him in a body bag. It was the undertaker, and his assistant who was so startled when Worky moved, that he dropped him.

Of course, after they came to their senses, they did take the real dead man away. ●

THE WETHERBEES

The Best New Hampshire Author

Judge "Plupy" Shute

WHO IS THE best author New Hampshire has produced?

Thomas Bailey Aldridge wrote about growing up in Portsmouth in the mid-eighteenth century. *The Story of a Bad Boy* is a classic.

Northwest Passage is a book by Kenneth Roberts about the exploits of Rogers' Rangers in the French and Indian Wars. Wonderfully written. Wonderful read.

Hey, how about *The Da Vinci Code?* Certainly author Dan Brown has proved to be the greatest seller of all time.

Speaking of bestsellers, how about Grace Metalious' *Peyton Place*? In its time, *Peyton Place* sold more copies than any other book except the Bible.

Back about the turn of the twentieth century, the best-selling author in America was a guy from Cornish named Winston Churchill. He was a different Churchill from the English prime minister during World War II. This Winston Churchill wrote dozens of books for the general public. His most popular was *Coniston*, a romantic comedy about the railroads and New Hampshire politics right after the Civil War. It's a page-turner.

All these authors and books are great, but my vote for the best New Hampshire writer goes to Plupy Shute.

What, never heard of Plupy Shute? Shame on you!

Thirty years ago Walter Cronkite wrote when he was growing up that everyone knew Plupy Shute was a better writer than Mark Twain!

And I agree.

Plupy Shute grew up in Exeter. He attended the local elementary schools and went to Philips Exeter and then to Harvard. Then he came back to town and set up practice as a lawyer.

For the rest of his life he lived in Exeter where he played in the Exeter Brass Band, served as judge of the police court and was a selectman.

My grandfather was a dentist and Judge Shute was one of his patients. Grandfather was very proud that he counted the judge as a personal friend.

The judge was born in 1856. He was named Henry Augustus Shute, but all the kids he grew up with called him "Plupy."

His best friends growing up were Pewt and Beany. They hiked the woods and swam in the rivers and fished and climbed and generally did mischief all over town.

We know this because one day the judge was up in his attic when he came across a diary that he had written when he was ten.

The judge was then also writing a column in the Exeter Newsletter.

Anyhow he published the diary with misspellings and all and

called it *The Real Diary of a Real Boy*. It soon became the best-selling book in America.

And, what do you know, Judge Shute went back to the attic and discovered a second diary he had written and he published that. He called it *Brite and Fare* for the first sentence of most of the entries. That, too, sold like hotcakes.

In the end, Plupy Shute published twenty volumes of diaries and reminiscences and one novel called *A Country Lawyer*.

All this time the judge kept his practice in law and was notorious for his easy-going attitude. Many of his clients couldn't or wouldn't pay him and he didn't care. He made a small fortune from his writing and that was enough.

Also he had a very sweet sense of humor based, not on irony, but rather on the absurdity of life . . . mostly his own.

He died in 1943 and all the businesses in Exeter closed for his funeral. He had not a single enemy in the world and thousands of friends.

Want proof? Read any one of his books. My favorite is the original. &

Bob Tagg

BOB TAGG AND his wife Phyllis lived upstairs in an apartment in my father's house.

Bob had been a Seabee in World War II, stationed in the South Pacific. He came home and had an earth-moving business. He was a surgeon when it came to operating a bulldozer blade. That being neither here nor there for this story, I just wanted to establish that this guy was a good guy and brave and smart.

But, about 1949, Bob Tagg broke a leg on a job site and was laid up in bed.

Well, I come from a large family, and in 1949 I turned thirteen and the other kids ranged in age from eight to three years old. We had a room for all the toys, and in this room was a new record player, one of those that automatically played records and which, if not stopped, would play the record again and again until someone stopped it.

The summer of 1949 was hot. And those were the days before air conditioning, and poor Bob Tagg was in his bed in traction in the room just above the toy room. He was uncomfortable, itchy and covered with sweat. It was horrible.

Well, this was the summer when the number-one hit song was "The Woody Woodpecker Song" . . . yah, the one in the cartoon. You may remember: "Ha, ha, he, haha," etc.

My brother Charlie loved the song and played it a lot. But often he would put it on the player and then go off with his friends. It wasn't vicious or anything. He was just a kid. He forgot.

You got it.

Bob Tagg's window was open and the window in the toy room was open and the music was loud.

Well, that day, my mom came home to hear Bob Tagg crying in agony for someone . . . anyone . . . to please, please, stop the music!

Dad took the record away from the kids so Bob would not have to hear it ever again. And that was the end of it.

Except . . . except that we also had all the Spike Jones records as well.

Charlie loved "Cocktails for Two." ✿

Bradford Springs

WHEN I WAS a teenager, I remember going deer hunting with my father over in the East Washington woods.

Afterwards, we went down a road and came to a drive, and at the end of the drive was a swamp, and in the swamp there was a boardwalk, at the end of which was a dilapidated hexagonal building, and in the building was a box, and in the box was a spring.

And the water in the spring, I remember, smelled of rotten eggs. What fun!

Dad said that he remembered when there was a terrific hotel nearby that people used to come to because of this spring that smelled like rotten eggs.

Well, as the years went by, the building over the spring rotted away and the road leading to it became more and more difficult to find.

I came back in the seventies with my own son and, at that time, there was nothing to show where the old spring used to be.

The spring is only about a mile from the center of East Washington, but it is located within the boundaries of Bradford.

There is a Native American legend that tells us they called this place "Big Medicine Water." The fact is, however, there is no proof it was ever called this or that the Native Americans ever used it.

They aren't sure who, of the settlers, rediscovered the spring, but the first time a person put a box over it was around 1820.

In 1844, one General Samuel Andrews of Hillsborough built a store, tannery and hotel in East Washington. Ten years later he built the first hotel near the sulfur spring. He called it "The Hermitage." It was forty-by-a-hundred feet long. (General Andrews was also the contractor of the Bradford and Claremont Railroad which brought guests to the hotel.)

In the 1890s a guy named Henry McCoy purchased the hotel and doubled its size, increasing the number of rooms to seventy-five. He called his hostelry The Bradford Springs Hotel. He built the octagonal house over the spring. He also added a bathhouse.

The hotel didn't serve booze. It was a spa. People went there for their health. They played croquet and rode horses, and hiked and bowled in the bowling alley, did marksmanship on the shooting range, and drank and bathed in the water of the stinky spring.

The water, according to the brochure from the hotel, was splendid for "cutaneous diseases" (which means skin problems). These diseases included eczema, erysipelas and scrofulodermas.

It also has cured, the brochure claimed, the worst forms of nasal catarrh, also catarrh of the stomach and bowels. Also catarrh of the mucous membranes of the gall ducts, bladder, throat, bronchial tubes. It was also splendid for dyspepsia and was an effective diuretic. Also inflammation of the eyes.

And for all that, guests were charged between six and ten dollars a week.

The Bradford Springs went the way of many of the grand hotels after the automobile came in and changed the way people estivated. Finally the place was torn down to avoid further taxes and an era came to a close.

And today?

Well, a few years ago the people in Bradford turned the area into a kind of park and hiking place. And there is a bulletin board with a description of the old hotel and other things that used to be there.

Nice place for a picnic. You might bring hard-boiled eggs. ❧

Fast Day

UNTIL A FEW years ago, the state of New Hampshire had an official holiday which was unique in the nation: Fast Day.

Fast Day was a day put aside for what used to be called "public humiliation," that is, the purging of the body and soul for the glory of God. On this day, one was supposed to eat less and not enjoy oneself at all. Church attendance was encouraged.

For this "public humiliation," the Lord was supposed to look kindly on one's labors and keep sickness from the home and bless the crops soon to be planted.

The first Fast Day in New Hampshire was in 1680, just when the province was separated from Massachusetts and became its own place.

New Hampshire was then ruled by a council of nine men. The president of that council was a merchant from Portsmouth, John Cutt, and he decided to get the new venture off to a flying start by calling for a Day of Public Humiliation.

But then the next spring John Cutt himself got sick and took to his bed. The rest of the council declared another day of fasting and prayer so Mr. Cutt might get better. Also people thought that the sighting of a comet a week or so before was a sign of God's displeasure, and so fasting and prayer was a good and safe course for the new province. The comet did not come back and neither did John Cutt. He died. He was sixty-eight.

Over the years there were a number of fasting days proclaimed, but people weren't joining in as much. In 1894 Massachusetts stopped its official Fast Day and substituted Patriots Day. Maine stopped its Fast Day three years later.

Five years later a bill to kill Fast Day came before the New Hampshire House. With great relish, not only did the legislative body not kill Fast Day, they made it an official holiday. It was the custom to have Fast Day on the last Thursday in April. Later on the legislature changed the day to the fourth Monday in April. People loved the holiday. But there wasn't much fasting.

When I was growing up, the day was mostly a time for going to

Boston for the sales. You see, it is only in recent times that stores were open on Sundays. In Manchester, for instance, even in the early 1960s you could not purchase, say, a can of peaches on Sunday. Anyone who sold anything other than perishables or newspapers on Sunday was arrested. True.

Now, as I say, Fast Day was not celebrated in Massachusetts. So the merchants in Boston took advantage of the fact that an entire state had a weekday off from work. And once a year they aimed their advertising directly at the Granite State. And people responded. Everyone, it seems, went to Boston on Fast Day to buy tires from Uncle Eff at Raymond's.

And so New Hampshire continued to be the only state in the union to celebrate a Fast Day. That is, until 1991. In 1991 the state replaced Fast Day with Civil Rights Day.

Now, I don't know about you, but I think it's a shame. I mean, I support Civil Rights Day, but I think we should have kept Fast Day as well.

Hey, it's good for the soul and, frankly, I could lose some weight. ✒

Refrigeration

I JUST RECENTLY bought a refrigerator.

I can't tell you the number of frozen dinners I have eaten over the last year.

Got me to thinking. What did we do before there was refrigeration?

Heck, my memories go back to icehouses. Hebby Miles had an icehouse right across the street from where I grew up in Milford. Every winter, back then, they'd harvest ice from Slab City Pond and over in Brookline at Potanapo Lake. In fact, the largest buildings in the area were the ice storage houses at Potanapo. Those ice storage houses on Slab City Pond lasted into the fifties.

My mother had an ice box when we lived up on High Street. Kept it out on the porch in the wintertime. There was this card with a number on each side: five, ten, fifteen, twenty. Mother would put it in the window with the size of the block of ice she wanted, and the ice man would drive up with a horse and wagon and, with a black rubber cape, would carry a piece of ice on his shoulder using his tongs. Every family I knew had ice tongs.

Everyone knew the iceman. Eugene O'Neil even wrote a play called "The Iceman Cometh." The play was about a guy who killed his wife because, he said, she was fooling around with the iceman. She wasn't and he was. Fooling around, that is (not with the iceman, of course). Oh this is getting way out of hand.

But even ice cut from a lake and packed in sawdust for use in the summertime was uncommon in the early days of America.

George Washington's brother sent a shipload of ice from Boston to Charleston, South Carolina, where they made the first ice cream most of the city had ever tasted. He lost money on that one.

But ice was not usually used in Colonial New England.

Of course they had corned beef and salted pork and codfish.

For fresh meat the settlers shared. One farmer would kill a pig or sheep or cow and would share the meat with his neighbors. Then a couple weeks later another farmer would slaughter an animal and share as well. This way there was fresh meat all year long. But meat was valuable stuff. Most meals did not include it.

The Hampton Falls Town History tells us that it wasn't until after the Civil War that butchers became popular in this country. Up 'til then it was neighbor to neighbor. ❧

Sauerkraut Slicer

DID I TELL you my dad was an inventor? Well, he was. Invented hundreds of things. Dad was a genuine craftsman. He was a cabinet-maker. Did wonderful finish work. Everything Dad built was beautifully crafted. Tight joints, plumb, like Norm Abram.

'Course, nothing Dad ever invented worked, but his projects always were built with wonderful craftsmanship. But they never worked.

A case in point: the sauerkraut slicer.

See, we (that is me and my brothers and sister) grew up in this big house on the corner of South and Clinton streets in Milford.

In the cellar Dad always had a fifteen-gallon crock filled with brine and cabbage. Dad loved sauerkraut and there was always a crock going.

Now the sauerkraut was always an embarrassment to us kids. We hated it. We couldn't get any friends to come home with us because of the sauerkraut. The smell would sidle up from the cellar into the kitchen. It was absolutely the most disgusting aroma imaginable. I could tell you what it smelled like but I couldn't put the words in print.

Anyhow, Dad decided that cutting the cabbage by hand was too labor-intensive. Besides, he had this vacuum-cleaner motor that came off our old Hoover.

An aside here: Remember Fibber McGee and Molly, the old radio show? Well, McGee used to plug the Hoover into the wall socket every week and get electrocuted. Everyone waited for the bit and everyone laughed. It was not a very good testimonial for Hoover but they didn't complain 'cause the mention of their name on the program sold millions of vacuum cleaners for 'em. Go figure.

Anyhow, Dad had this perfectly good vacuum-cleaner motor and he set about building a sauerkraut slicer using the motor as the base. Now this wasn't a bad idea. Later someone would create the food processor, which did the same thing and before that there was the Veg-o-Matic (I know, you are too young to remember the Veg-o-Matic; that is, unless you remember Fibber McGee).

Anyhow, the invention was very like those that would come later. Dad used an old fan belt from his 1946 Dodge truck and he built the slicer body of plywood and the blades were hand-ground and bolted to a circular thingy.

So on a cold winter night we all gathered in the kitchen to witness Dad's sauerkraut slicer. Pop took a head of cabbage and wedged it into the square slot in the front of the contraption. He then turned on the motor. It was loud. How loud? About as loud as a chain saw without a muffler.

Now, not only could the neighbors smell us from the street, they also had to cease conversation as they ran by because of the noise.

The cabbage head just sat there. Then Dad lifted up this wooden poker thingy. He presented it much like a magician shows his audience that there is nothing in his hat. Dad was, if nothing else, a showman.

In the plunger went and out the doors of the kitchen went the family. It was a disaster. The machine shredded the cabbage into teeny, tiny particles and blew them all over the kitchen. It was a veritable snowstorm. We all had shredded cabbage in our eyebrows, in our hair, in our socks, yes, in our underwear. There was cabbage in the light fixtures, the stove, all over the ceiling. We didn't see the cat for days.

Mother was pleased because Dad re-painted her kitchen, ceiling and all. And the sauerkraut slicer was put on a shelf amid the redolence of the basement to lie there for years unused, until one day Dad decided to use the old motor for another invention . . . but that's a story for another time. ⟡

Snow Sculpture

BOY, WHEN WE are young we do some stupid things.

The other day I got an e-mail from Bill McGee reminding me of one of those things. Bill, by the way, was my best friend in Milford High School. This was about 1950. Wintertime. A weekend. We were, let's see . . . in 1950, we were thirteen or fourteen.

Bill and I had been pegging snowballs at my little brothers and, generally, having a wonderful time that day.

"Hey, help me with this." Bill was rolling a big snowball across the front lawn. We pushed a second ball and put it on top, and then a third. Pretty neat snowman. Couldn't find anything for eyes. Then Bill said, "How about this?" and he added an extra dimension to the snow sculpture.

"Wow," I said.

See, it was no longer a snowman; it was definitely a snow woman.

The snow that day was pretty sticky and we were able to augment our *objet d'art* to stunning proportions there in the middle of the lawn.

People going by began to respond. There were lots of honks from cars. We were a success!

We continued for an hour or so more refining the features, as it were, of our Venus, and now people were rolling down their car windows and yelling, "Oh, Yah!" as they passed . . . at least the male drivers were. We were in hysterics rolling around in the snow on the lawn. Never had so much fun.

Until we looked up and my Mom was standing on the porch looking at our creation.

"Hi, Mom!"

"Doing an art project?" she asked.

Bill wanted to melt into the snow. He was an Eagle Scout, after all, and, somehow, he knew this was not in the Scout manual.

"Push that thing over," Mom said. "People are calling me on the phone about it."

"Oh," we were stunned.

"Right now!" she said and we went behind our beautiful creation and pushed her over, face first. She only went about four feet before she got hung up.

We then kicked her into oblivion.

Both Bill and I felt like serial killers.

But next day we're the talk of the school. Everyone knew of our artistry and we were heroes . . . in a sort of a Beavis and Butt-Head way. ✎

Thumbing

Looks odd, doesn't it? Hitchhiking. No one hitchhikes any more. When you see someone with their thumb out nowadays, you just pass on by. Gotta be something wrong.

But there was a time when it was odd if you didn't see a hitchhiker when you were on a main road.

In the Sixties and early Seventies, millions of people hitchhiked. And you'd pick them up usually if they met the profile. That profile included an age limit . . . the perimeter was junior high school through college age. Anyone younger was hardly ever seen. But older hitchhiking was okay if the costume looked right. The costume was bib overalls and sandals or bare feet. Hippies. If you were older and dressed this way, I guarantee a Volkswagen bus would stop within a few minutes. And there were thousands of Volkswagen buses.

I used to hitchhike in the Army. In fact, the summer of 1959 I hitchhiked home to Milford from Fort Belvoir, Virginia, every single weekend . . . left on Friday . . . got back for roll call on Monday. Every single weekend except one.

That one was when I got picked up by the MPs in New Jersey and put in jail for the night. It was the only time I ever spent in a jail cell, and it was worth it. I think we all ought to experience everything we can, short of hurting other people.

In high school, we used to hitchhike to Nashua from Milford to go to the movies. Nothing was thought of it . . . at least by my parents.

Now Bill McGee's parents, that's another story. See, Bill was an only child and an Eagle Scout and an "A" student. His parents frowned on any hitch-hiking and, moreover, they discouraged his friendship with me.

Anyhow, it was late summer about 19 . . . mmm . . . 52, I'd say, and Bill McGee and I were bored silly. We were hanging around downtown Milford and nothing was happening.

So I had an idea. Why, I said, don't we hitchhike . . . put our thumbs out . . . and whoever stops, let's ask him where he is going . . . and go there? An adventure.

So we spit on our hands and shook on it.

I said, "No chickening out. I know you, McGee, and you are a candy-something when it comes to taking chances."

"I won't chicken out," he said.

Now, like I say, Bill McGee was an Eagle Scout, a real one, and a Scout doesn't lie, and so I knew he would not go back on his word.

We put our thumbs out and right off a car stopped. The car was driven by Russ Brown. Russ was in the Navy and he was headed back to Quonset Point, Rhode Island.

So we went to Quonset Point, and it took us all night to hitchhike back.

In the meantime, our parents were in touch with the police who had an APB out for us.

When we arrived back in Milford, Bill's parents were not speaking to my parents and Bill was confined to his home for an entire month.

Bill's mother died a while ago . . . she was in her nineties and, I am told, she had forgiven me. ❧

Wet Wipes

THIS STORY HAPPENED about forty-four years ago. We were driving into Milford from Wilton. "We" was my wife of the time and my son, Caleb, who was then about six.

It was winter and there was snow, and it was still snowing and there was very little visibility. Just up the hill past the old Heywood Farms ice cream restaurant, there was some roadwork going on and as we came to it we almost ran into a woman standing in the snow.

She was an older woman in a housedress and she was attempting to change a tire there in the wet snow and mud.

As I swerved around her, I said to Hilda, "That looks like your mother."

We stopped, and I went back. Sure enough it was Mary Berwick, and she was having one heck of a time trying to loosen up the lug nuts on the tires. I escorted her back to our car and went back with a flashlight to finish changing her tire. The nuts were rusted on and I had to stand on the wrench to loosen them. I got the tire on and went back to my car where there was a big ruckus going on. I shined my light in the window.

My mother-in-law looked a mess. She and Hilda were, however, laughing uproariously.

Seems Mary had gotten into the car and her daughter had fished around in the glove compartment for a couple of those Wet Wipes that are in foil packages. Mary was grateful for the heat and to be able to get clean. But then she said, "Oh my!" and "Oh my!" And no one knew what had happened 'til I shined the flashlight in the window.

Seems Hilda had given her mother not Wet Wipes, but rather a couple packages of fast-food ketchup.

So that's the story.

And you know, every time I tell that story, I get a hankering for French fries. ✒

The Gage Girls

I HAVE BEEN driving past Gage Girls Road in Bedford for fifty years now. And yes, I have had a driver's license for over fifty years, and for all that time I have wondered, as perhaps you have, "Who the heck are or were the Gage girls? And why 'girls?' Why not 'women?'"

As a teenager I fantasized about the Gage girls. They had to be, in my mind, blondes, with rosy cheeks and large welcoming bosoms. And, if we ever met, they would love me forever, and I would be unable to choose between them. And we would grow old, alas, never consummating our love . . . or better yet, well, I won't go into my fantasies because, because it's none of your business.

Alas, the Gage girls and I never met. And, over the years, no one in Bedford could tell me who the Gage girls were. I always asked whenever I found out someone was from Bedford, just in case. But, like I say, no one ever knew.

Recently an old high school friend of mine, Bill McGee, e-mailed me to ask if I ever found out who the Gage girls were. I sheepishly had to admit that I still didn't know.

So I went to the Bedford Town History.

OK. Out this road about a quarter mile is the homestead of the Gage family. They are some of the earliest settlers of the town. McIntosh Gage was the settler who first built a home on the road. His brother, William, lived with him.

The house burned down and William built a second house about a hundred yards away from the first one. He died and left the property to his son, also William, and two daughters. Sarah was born in 1861, and Addie was a born in 1866. Well, the brother died young, thirty-two years old, and the two sisters lived alone in the house until their death sometime in the 1950s, I understand, when they were in their nineties. They never married.

In the mid-fifties the post office required that all roads be given a name and this road was always referred to as the place where the Gage girls grew up. They died about that time and, probably out of nostalgia, the selectmen voted to call the road after them.

I have not been able to find a photograph of the Gage girls, so I don't know what they looked like when they were young. But in 1952, when I was daydreaming about them, I may have had a better romantic chance than I thought. ❧

A Few of My Favorite Things

"HERE ARE," AS the song says, "a few of my favorite things." A few:

My favorite city is Portsmouth. I lived there half a dozen years and found it to have the amenities of a big city and to be as handleable as a small town. My favorite historical house in Portsmouth is the Macpheadris-Warner House.

Macpheadris-Warner House

My favorite theater is the Palace in Manchester.

The Palace in Manchester

Best movie theater is the Town Hall Theater in Wilton. For smaller venues, I like the Newport Opera House, the Claremont Opera

House, and the Rochester Opera House. But, perhaps best of all is the Littleton Opera House. Bette Davis once had a birthday party there.

Town Hall Theater in Wilton

Newport Opera House

Claremont Opera House

Rochester Opera House

Littleton Opera House

For sports, of course, it's the Verizon Center in Manchester and the Whittemore Center in Durham.

Favorite ballpark is Holman Stadium in Nashua. The terrific Fisher Cats stadium in Manchester isn't old enough yet.

For skiing: Cannon Mountain.

Best swimming hole is in Meriden by the covered bridge there. Problem is, this is a town park and only open to residents.

The Meriden swimming hole

Favorite public swimming place is at Bear Trail on the Kancamagus Highway out of Conway.

Favorite natural gorge is Lost River.

Favorite profile is Indian Head.

In my opinion the prettiest large lake in the state is Newfound Lake. Squam Lake is wonderful. And, of course, Winnipesaukee is the most spectacular. My favorite small lake and, not incidentally, fishing lake, is Nubanusit Lake in Hancock; it's also in Nelson. The first Connecticut Lake is on my list, too.

My favorite hotel is the Mt. Washington with the Balsams a very close second. I also love the Mountain View in Whitefield and Wentworth by the Sea in New Castle.

The Mt. Washington Hotel, Bretton Woods

My favorite covered bridge is up in Stark. The most impressive covered bridge is the Cornish-Windsor Bridge. My favorite steel bridge is the Oxford-Fairlee Bridge. And my favorite footbridge is the Milford Swinging Bridge.

The Stark covered bridge

New Hampshire's longest and shortest bridges, the Cornish-Windsor Bridge spanning the Connecticut River and the Prentiss Bridge in Langdon

My favorite town hall on the outside is in Walpole. And my favorite town hall inside is in Middleton.

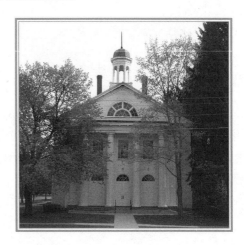

Walpole Town Hall

Best meetinghouse is in Sandown.
The best library is in Peterborough.

The Sandown meetinghouse

The Peterborough Town Library

My favorite cemetery is in Jaffrey Center. This is the cemetery where the former slave Amos Fortune is buried and also author Willa Cather.

My favorite gravestone is the one for Samuel Jones' leg in Washington. Second favorite is the Carrie Cutter grave in the Elm Street Cemetery in Milford. Her stone states that she was murdered by the Baptist Church.

The prettiest small towns in New Hampshire are, in my opinion, Harrisville, Haverhill, Hancock, Hillsboro Center, and Hopkinton. All begin with the letter "H." Amherst is pretty neat, too. And, oh my gosh, the town of Washington takes my breath away.

But when it all comes down to it, I'd be hard-pressed to find a more perfect town than Walpole.

My favorite gift shops are at the New Hampshire Historical Society, and the Audubon Society in Concord. Also the shops at the Manchester Historic Association and Currier Gallery of Art and the Hopkins Center at Dartmouth have stuff you can't find other places.

The Currier is my favorite art museum. The Hood in Hanover is an international treasure as well. For a natural history museum the Woodman in Dover wins hands down.

Favorite mountain is Chocorua.

Favorite thing that most people have never visited is the Madison Boulder.

And favorite event has to be the Gilsum Rock Swap.

My most favorite New Hampshire celebrity is, of course, Judson Hale, publisher emeritus of *Yankee Magazine* . . . with Adam Sandler a distant second.

So, there you have my favorite fishing place, swimming place, skiing place, my favorite towns, my favorite everything. That is the story. ✒

If you enjoyed this book, you will also enjoy:

Fritz Wetherbee's New Hampshire
ISBN 978-0-9755216-5-6 / $19.95

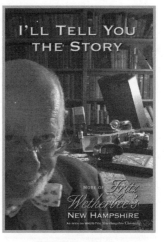

I'll Tell You the Story
ISBN 978-0-9755216-9-4 / $19.95

More Stories from
New Hampshire Chronicle
ISBN 978-0-9790784-5-3 / $19.95

PLAIDSWEDE PUBLISHING
www.plaidswede.com